FROM THE MAN WHO MAKES DREAMS COME TRUE...

Request:

Dear Mr. Ross:

Ever since I was little, I always wanted to be a fashion model. I've done some modeling locally and friends tell me I am attractive and photogenic.

I've made many, many sacrifices and denied myself luxuries to save $300 toward a trip to New York, where I hope to be interviewed for a career in modeling.

Can you possibly arrange an interview for me at the Wilhelmina Agency or the Ford Modeling Agency?

I want a good future for myself, Mr. Ross. Will you please help me get started?

H.L. Chicago, Illinois

Answer:

Percy Ross telephoned William Weinberg, president of the Wilhelmina Agency and then paid for her round-trip expenses to the Big Apple.

Request:

Dear Mr. Ross:

Since you're being so darn generous I am not at all embarrassed as I ask for the following: farm in the country, Rolls Royce, yacht (150 ft), Swiss bank account of five figures, wardrobe from Saks, and a motorbike.

Being a millionaire, you can easily afford my dream list.

S.U. Santa Ana, Calif.

Answer:

Dear S.,

Your List is too big for me. I'm a millionaire, not a billionaire. Try Santa Claus.

P9-CFT-091

Most Berkley Books are available at special quantity discounts for bulk purchases for sales promotions, premiums, fund raising, or educational use. Special books or book excerpts can also be created to fit specific needs.

For details, write or telephone Special Markets, The Berkley Publishing Group, 200 Madison Avenue, New York, New York 10016; (212) 686-9820.

THE SECRET OF GETTING WHAT YOU WANT BY KNOWING HOW TO ASK FOR THE MOON—AND GET IT!

PERCY ROSS
WITH DICK SAMSON

B

BERKLEY BOOKS, NEW YORK

To protect the privacy of a few individuals whose letters have been published in this book, different names or initials and geographic locations may have been substituted.

This Berkley book contains the complete
text of the original hardcover edition.

ASK FOR THE MOON—AND GET IT!

A Berkley Book / published by arrangement with
the author

PRINTING HISTORY
G. P. Putnam's Sons edition / January 1987
Berkley edition / October 1987

All rights reserved.
Copyright © 1987 by Percy Ross.
This book may not be reproduced in whole or in part,
by mimeograph or any other means, without permission.
For information address: The Berkley Publishing Group,
200 Madison Avenue, New York, NY 10016.

ISBN: 0-425-10336-6

A BERKLEY BOOK ® TM 757,375
Berkley Books are published by The Berkley Publishing Group,
200 Madison Avenue, New York, NY 10016.
The name "BERKLEY" and the "B" logo
are trademarks belonging to Berkley Publishing Corporation.

PRINTED IN THE UNITED STATES OF AMERICA

10   9   8   7   6   5   4   3   2   1

To those with impossible dreams, real needs, or simple desires . . . and to all who have hesitated to reach out:

I dedicate this book.

Contents

Part I

GETTING READY

Chapter 1

How to Ask
for the Moon

My life has seen the fulfillment of two dreams. The first dream, which I pursued from early childhood, was to become a millionaire. I made that dream come true by working hard and by learning how to ask people for help. I was able to convince friends, family, employers, bankers, customers, and others to assist with a thousand small things that contributed, bit by bit, to my success in business—and in life.

The second dream was to share my wealth with those who are less fortunate. I wanted to give encouragement, hope, spirit, and money—to show people that somebody cared about them and their future.

I began living that dream, full-time, in the early 1970s. Through my column, "Thanks a Million," which is syndicated in over 140 newspapers, I've been able to give help and support to thousands of others throughout the United States. Many people write asking me for assistance every week, and I have a full-time staff to help answer their requests.

Though my philanthropy involves giving, it has taught me much about the art of asking. Over the years I have received many, many requests for money, goods, or assistance of one type or another. Most of the time, the reason I answer "yes" instead of "no" is that the person asks *in the right way* for something that is needed. He or she has discovered the winning principles of asking. That knowledge can help you too get whatever you want in every area of your life—at work or school, at home or in your community.

THE SECRET TO GETTING WHAT YOU WANT

I believe that if you ask, and ask in the right way, you can have whatever you want in life: wealth, material goods, happiness, rich life experiences, fulfilling relationships, and more.

Knowing how to ask can bring you a raise, investment capital to start a business of your own, the job you've always wanted, more responsibility, a willing audience for your ideas, a better price for things you want to buy, the cooperation of family members or fellow employees, moral support when you face difficulties, rich new friendships, even expensive possessions you thought you could never afford.

British novelist and philosopher Aldous Huxley once said, "People always get what they ask for." Much earlier, Jesus proclaimed, "Ask, and it shall be given you."

Asking *can* help make your dearest dreams come true. But there's an art to asking. The goal of this book is to teach you that art.

FROM RAGS TO RICHES THROUGH ASKING

When I was just six years old, growing up in Laurium in the copper mining region of Michigan's Upper Peninsula, I asked my father for a bicycle. He looked at me sadly, and shook his head. My parents, immigrants from Latvia and Russia, had nothing. They could not afford any extras. Other kids had bicycles, but it was all my parents could do to keep us warm and fed. My parents cared about us kids, and they did the very best they could. Still, I wanted a bike, and I wanted one badly. As I walked along the dusty roadside, I envied the wealthy mining company officials who drove by in their plush automobiles.

It was then that I first decided that wealth would bring me some of the things I dreamed of. I set my sights on becoming a millionaire.

It may sound absurd or outlandish, but never underestimate the power of setting goals—and pursuing them. It can work miracles, even for a poor, bikeless, but hopeful kid. My dreams came true, and then some. I asked life to make me a millionaire. Life made me a multimillionaire.

I asked for the moon and got it. You can too. I attribute my success to sacrifice, dedication, hard work, a little luck—and a whole lot of asking. I would not be where I am if I had not convinced many, many people to help me along the way.

MY FIRST LESSONS

At a very early age, I had to help my family earn money by asking people to buy things from me. My dad bought me a crate of eggs (36 dozen) from a farmer and told me to go from house to house and ask the neighbors to buy them. I was six or seven at the time. It was my first selling job. It taught me to sell Percy Ross, as well as a product. I learned to smile, to be pleasant, to talk to people—as a way to earn a little money.

I did quite well. Within a year I had regular customers and was selling three crates a week, delivering them in my small wagon or sled, depending on the season. My father told me to give my customers an extra egg every once in a while, so I did. You'd think I was giving them an extra dozen! I earned many loyal customers that way. I've never forgotten his advice: "Always give your customers a little more than they expect." My success in selling eggs taught me an important lesson: Asking and giving go together.

My father was a peddler, junk dealer, and jack-of-all-trades. Through his coaching and example, I became a survivor, and I learned to make my way in the world. My father helped me keep a positive attitude. "Don't give up, Percy," he used to say.

I worked alongside him in many of his business ventures: buying and selling junk, running a secondhand furniture and clothing store, selling army surplus supplies, peddling fruits and vegetables, selling ice cream for 5 cents a cone. He went broke, or barely squeaked by, in all of these businesses; but I grew richer in knowledge.

As I got a little older, I saw my dad make his first real money buying and selling junk. I'll never forget the first time I went along with him to sell a truckload of junk in Milwaukee. He had been paying 2 cents a pound for scrap copper and brass. My mother, two brothers, and I had the job of separating the iron handles from the copper kettles and the wooden handles from the aluminum pots and pans. We then pounded the metal flat to get more in our truck.

When my father and I got to Milwaukee, I saw with my own eyes that we could get 4 cents a pound for junk metal that we bought for 2 cents. Lights flashed and bells rang in my head. I was hooked; I had received my baptism in the profit motive. I now knew how to travel the road to riches: Ask people to sell things to me at one price; ask others to buy those things from me at another, higher price; and contribute something—pound out the metal, shape a desirable product—in between the two transactions. I remember telling myself this was an exciting game I wanted to play. I've never stopped feeling that way.

During this period I also learned valuable lessons about asking through another kind of activity—trying to collect money from people who were in debt to my father. My mother was my mentor in this. She taught me how to stand tall, smile, and ask politely but earnestly for payment. I learned to do it with pride, respect, and friendly persistence. The money I brought in—a goodly amount—helped keep food on our table in those lean years.

TEENAGE UPS AND DOWNS

When I was about eighteen, I started rebuilding junk batteries. It was the first business I started and ran totally on my own. I talked junkyard operators into selling me old batteries for 25 to 30 cents apiece. Batteries in those days had three cells; when a battery went bad, there would always be one or two good cells left. So I'd take all the good cells, put them together, and make a good battery. Then I would put on my salesman's hat. I convinced people that rebuilt batteries were good in spite of their junkyard origins, and I got about $2.75 for each one. I made about $100 a month—a lot of money then. It was a real triumph for me.

When I was still in high school, there was so much poverty that boys and unemployed men would go into the mines and mills at night and steal scrap metal from mining property that was being torn down. As my dad was still in the junk business, they'd come to us to sell it. I didn't realize that I was guilty of buying contraband merchandise, and soon I got in trouble with the law.

If ever I needed to use the power of persuasion, I needed it then. I asked the mining property owner who confronted me, Mr. Davis, to give me another chance. I must have said something right, because he agreed. Not only did he drop the charges, but later he offered me a job with the Duluth Hide & Fur Company, and the West End Iron and Metal Company, which I accepted.

That summer I left home to work with Mr. Davis in Duluth. My father told me, "You didn't do very well in high school, and we can't afford to send you to college. Here's your chance for an education that money can't buy." And quite an education it was too! In addition to learning the ins and outs of two businesses—scrap-metal and furs and hides—I progressively developed my ability to talk people into things. Traveling all over the country, I learned how to wheel and deal with junk dealers and trappers. I even mastered the quick-talk skills of auctioneering.

THREE FAILURES AND ONE GREAT SUCCESS

I worked for Mr. Davis and his partner for six years, until after World War II. In 1946 I decided to go into business for myself; I thought I was ready for it. I was married and had a baby boy. We moved to Minneapolis and I organized the Northwest Fur Auction Company with $100,000 I had managed to save.

To get the business going, I had to do a lot of persuading, naturally. The biggest thing I needed was cooperation from the fur dealers and mink ranchers. Seventy percent of all the furs sold in America originated in my part of the country, but they were shipped to New York or Seattle for auction. I asked the dealers and ranchers to send their furs to me in Minneapolis.

I must have been very persuasive, because many agreed to do so. Then I asked the New York buyers to come to me—and they did! The fur auction business—or a big chunk of it—shifted to the source of supply, the heartlands. And I had a thriving company on my hands.

Sometime later, though, I ran into trouble. The fur trading industry started doing badly, and my 5-percent commission just wasn't enough to keep my family fed and clothed. In five years, I was broke. To add insult to injury, a New York dealer gave me a bad check for $25,000. This was my first big failure. After paying off all I owed, I had nothing left.

17

For the next eight years I ran auctions for heavy construction equipment, such as bulldozers, all over the country. I did quite well. Then fierce competition reared its ugly head and I got involved in several costly lawsuits. That put me out of business. I failed big a second time.

Though broke, I still had a good reputation. I asked a bank to lend me $30,000 to buy a small, financially troubled manufacturer of polyethylene plastic bags. The bank said yes. I changed the firm's name from Indian Head Plastics to Poly-Tech Corporation, and moved it from Eau Claire, Wisconsin, to Bloomington, Minnesota.

In spite of all my efforts, the business did poorly. Within four years, Poly-Tech was half a million dollars in the red, and I had no choice but to file for reorganization under Chapter 11 of the U.S. Bankruptcy Court. Once again I was broke. I had failed for the third time.

Then I remembered my father, his struggles, and his advice to me. Was I going to give up? Something in me stiffened; my will became hard and unyielding, like a piece of my father's scrap iron.

I decided not to let Poly-Tech go under, but to bring it back and make it profitable. To accomplish that, I needed all my powers of persuasion, more than I had ever needed them before.

After selling off everything my family could possibly get along without, I asked my wife, Laurian, and my two sons, Steven and Larry, to help me with the business. They did. I asked many lending institutions to put up working capital in spite of the bankruptcy proceedings. All but one said no, but one was all I needed. I asked my creditors to cooperate and wait for their money; enough of them agreed to enable me to go on. I asked my employees to think of ways to streamline production and sales, and they came through.

Within three years we had turned the tide. We repaid all our debts, and business began to boom. Three years later, in 1969, U.S. Industries offered to buy me out. I asked for $8 million—and got it.

The day I received the check from U.S. Industries was the same day the Apollo astronauts landed on the moon—July 20, 1969. The coincidence still amazes me. I asked for the moon and got it on the same day humanity got the real moon after John Kennedy asked for *it*. President Kennedy had asked Congress to appropriate funds for manned space flight in 1961. He asked space scientists, engineers, technicians, administrators, suppliers, and astronauts to take on an "impossible" task. And he asked taxpaying citizens to support a ten-year program that offered little prospect of economic reward. He asked the nation—he asked all of us—to give him the moon, and we gave it to him!

Having achieved the personal "moon" I had dreamed of for so many years—becoming a millionaire—I began to consolidate my wealth and shift course toward my second dream, becoming a philanthropist. I divided the $8 million equally between my wife, my two sons, and myself. I invested my own $2 million in over a hundred ventures ranging from Broadway shows to oil wells, Hollywood movies to copper mines. I lost most of my investments. Fortunately, two of the ventures paid off handsomely. I amassed many millions, enough to realize my second dream.

LET A GIVER GUIDE YOUR ASKING

With my wealth, I now had the chance to help people, as others had helped me. In the winter of 1977 I heard of the plight of fifty Vietnamese refugees, and I made available $50,000 to help them reach the United States and start a new life.

I remember reading that John D. Rockefeller had given dimes to children early in this century. I decided to do the same thing with silver dollars. I tossed 16,500 of them to children at the Aquatennial Parade in Minneapolis in the summer of 1978. I gave 10,000 more at a parade in Wabasha, Minnesota, the next year. Since then I have distributed as many as 100,000 silver dollars per year. To me, the silver dollar symbolizes the American dream of financial success that is possible for any person who dares to act on that dream.

I have now come to the aid of many individuals in need. My aim has been to make a difference in their lives if I possibly can. For example, a young girl who was dying of cancer wanted a horse, but her parents couldn't afford one. So I arranged for a beautiful pony to be delivered at her doorstep the day before Christmas. A boy who was dying of cancer wanted a swing set. I made that dream come true too. The amazing thing is that both of these kids are still alive today. This, perhaps, means more to me than anything.

Over the years, the word spread that an unusual millionaire named Percy Ross gave money away to ordinary individuals. People started writing me, asking for things. I said yes as often as I could.

As a result of these requests, in 1983 I began writing

my syndicated newspaper column, "Thanks a Million." This exposure brought a tremendous amount of mail. Hundreds of readers began asking me for advice and material aid—money, a stove, eyeglasses, a bicycle, whatever they needed.

I now receive up to 8,000 letters every week from people requesting aid. Through these letters, as well as through the lessons I learned in my life, I've developed a great deal of insight into how to make successful requests—in other words, how to ask for what you want *and get it.* I've learned that if you reach out to others in the right way, you have a much better chance of gaining what you want in life. I can't stress this point too strongly.

In my philanthropy, I help as many people as possible, but of course I can't help everyone. I've got to pick and choose among the many requests I receive as a result of my column. And I have my reasons for saying "yes" or "no." In the pages that follow you'll find out why I said:

- yes to five women who asked for mink coats
- no to a woman who asked for help with her relationship with her husband
- yes to a twenty-seven-year-old woman who asked for a pickup truck.

IF YOU ASK, AND ASK IN THE RIGHT WAY, ANYTHING IS POSSIBLE

If you ask for what you need and want in life, you just might get it. That's my basic advice. If you don't ask for much, you probably won't get much. If you don't ask people for the help or favors or money you need, you probably won't get it.

You've got to ask! Asking is, in my opinion, the world's most powerful—and neglected—secret to success and happiness. A friend of mine, John Stone, created a multimillion-dollar corporation from scratch, practically single-handedly. He now consults with business leaders. As this book was being prepared, he and I had a discussion about how important making requests is to business success. "You know," he said, "without doing a lot of asking every day, there's no way I could have succeeded. In fact, I couldn't even have *started* my company."

Most people don't fully appreciate the fact that no matter who you are, if you want something in life, you've got to learn to ask for it.

You've got to ask in the right way, though. You can't simply make requests any old way and expect results. You must first learn the who, what, where, when, why, and how of reaching out. This book will teach you. It will give you the tools to ask successfully, and show you how other people have used them. As you read, you'll find out how:

- an out-of-work young man with less than $6 to his name persuaded a stranger three thousand miles away to wire him $400
- a harried mother got her unruly young children to start cooperating
- a famous actress changed a "no" into the big break she needed
- a family with a modest income convinced the

world's most famous architect to design the home of their dreams—at a cost they could afford.

The heart of this book is made up of what I call the ten rules of asking. By using these ten rules, anyone, I believe, can increase his or her chances of getting a "yes" to almost any request.

Learning how to ask has made me richer than my wildest dreams, and happier than I dared hope. If asking can do this for the son of a poor immigrant junk dealer, then think what it can do for you! Asking for the moon *works*.

KNOWING HOW TO ASK IS NOT MAGIC

The principles of asking bring proven results. But they are not magic. They don't work in every situation. You're not going to get a "yes" every time you make a request—even if you ask in the right way.

I've been turned down many times in my life. But I've always taken my father's motto to heart: "Don't give up! Don't *ever* give up!"

HOW TO BENEFIT MOST

My ten rules of asking are deceptively simple, but very powerful—more powerful than you might imagine. If you apply these rules, your life may never be the same again.

Beware of one danger, however. Too many readers of self-improvement books fall into the "read-only" trap. They enjoy reading and dreaming, they appreciate the tips and pointers, they even learn a few things; but they *do* little or nothing to attain their goals. Success comes not just from fantasizing about success, but from your follow-through. This is especially true of some highly educated people who intellectualize but never seem to actualize.

You won't get the moon just by reading. Before continuing with this book, ask yourself this question: "Am I willing to apply the basic rules of asking in my daily life?"

If your answer is "yes," you've already taken the first step in realizing your dreams.

Chapter 2

How Would You
Answer These Requests?

As an introduction to the rules of asking—and to getting what you want—I invite you to consider how *you* react when different kinds of requests are made of *you*. Why do you say "yes" sometimes and "no" other times?

The following situations will let you play decision maker. Decide how *you* would answer each request—and why. Then read on to find out what actually happened in real life.

Situation #1: Lower Expenses and Higher Pay

Suppose you're Mr. Beck, owner of a fur trading company. You buy pelts from dealers, and sell them to coat manufacturers. Business is okay, but not great. In order to boost profits, you've got to reduce expenses. Cost cutting—that's what preoccupies you these days.

One afternoon a young employee comes to you and says: "Mr. Beck, I've been working here more than two years, and I haven't had a raise. I want to get married, and I sure could use more money . . ."

What would you say?

* * *

If you said "yes," you're probably a very nice person. I might say yes too. But wouldn't you agree that Mr. Beck might see little justification for an increase? What's in it for him besides yet higher costs? The young man neglected an important rule of asking. Luckily, when I was in the same situation, I made my request keeping Rule #4 (which I explain in Chapter 6) in mind. As a result, I got my raise and got married.

If you apply the same rule, you'll find that you will get many of the things you ask for.

Situation #2: Yard Work

Suppose you're a retired gentleman who enjoys gardening and mowing the lawn. A twelve-year-old boy who lives in another part of town knocks on your door one day. "I'm looking for yard work," he says. You tell him thanks anyway, but you don't need any help.

The next week he walks by your house while you're trimming a hedge. "Sure you don't need any help?" he asks. You explain that you enjoy doing the work yourself, and you suggest he try some of the neighbors down the street.

Three days later he walks by your house again. This time you are pulling weeds from a flowerbed. He asks the names of the flowers, and you tell him. He watches you work for awhile, asking a question now and then. Finally he says, "Looks like you got a lot of weeds. I'm good at pulling weeds."

Do you think the boy got the job?

* * *

In fact, the retired gentleman—a former news reporter—did hire the boy. They worked together for many a weekend, becoming fast friends.

The rule the boy applied, Rule #9, which I describe in Chapter 11, is so basic that many people overlook it. If you neglect this rule, your chances of success may be nil.

Situation #3: "$25,000 by This Friday!"

My longtime associate, Connie Hanson, received the following phone call one morning from a reader who had written me with a request for money (Connie had arrived at work, by the way, at 8:30, half an hour early, when she got the call): "Where have you been? I've been trying to reach you for two hours! I wrote Mr. Ross a letter last week and told him I needed $25,000 by this Friday, and I haven't heard a word from him."

If *you* were the person who had to decide whether to grant or deny the woman's request, what would *your* response be?

* * *

In this case, the rule the caller violated (Rule #7, described in Chapter 9) is quite obvious. Yet most of us violate this rule in more subtle ways, without realizing it. Once we correct this error, other people will stop rejecting us automatically and begin to feel more open to our requests.

Situation #4: An International Dilemma

Several decades ago, a young lady, still in her teens, somehow managed to talk her way into the office of the president of Liberia. Her palms were sweaty and she was trembling as she blurted out her request. She explained that she had won a scholarship to an American university, but did not have the money to pay for transportation. If she could not get to America, she would have to give up her scholarship. She asked if the government could give her $200 for a boat ticket plus a little extra money to pay off some small debts.

The president replied, "The government allows grants to medical students. Are you studying medicine?"

The color drained from her face. Her reply was very faint. "No, Mr. President, I want to study law." There was a long silence.

If you were the president, what would you do?

* * *

In fact, the president replied, "Perhaps we could make an exception. Would it help if we gave you $500?" The young lady, Angie Brooks, went on to become president of the United Nations General Assembly in 1969.

Angie Brooks applied several rules of effective asking. One in particular, Rule #5 (see Chapter 7), came through loud and clear. This principle is like dynamite in a gold mine; it can blast your way to wealth.

Situation #5: Raising Children and Money
The following letter was sent to me in care of a newspaper that runs my "Thanks a Million" column:

Dear Mr. Ross,

My mother has raised 11 children. All are grown and on their own. She has worked hard all her life and helps everybody else before helping herself.

She is unable to work except at home. Her hobby is dolls. She wants to make some money by learning doll design and doll repair from a school in California. Enrollment is $345. Can you help her?

I. R.
Fort Wayne, Indiana

The situation described in the letter isn't as simple as it sounds. If you were in my shoes, what would you do?

* * *

Here was my response:

Dear I. R.,

Things are cheaper by the dozen. Your mother has 11 children. Pretend I'm number 12! I'll pay $1/12$ of the enrollment cost. That's $28.75 for each of us. OK?

Obviously I wanted to help. But why did I offer to contribute so little? Was I simply being cheap?

No. When I read, "My mother has raised 11 children," a loud buzzer went off in my head. One of the principles of making a request was being blatantly violated.

If you apply Rule #2 (described in Chapter 4) as you go after what you want in life, you will save yourself a lot of time. You will also, in many cases, double, triple, or even quadruple your odds of success. In my business dealings, I have more than once used this principle to turn certain defeat into a victory.

Situation #6: Getting to Yes

A young Kansas man was turned down several times by the girl he wanted to marry. Then one day he got a bright idea, and took his harvester out into a large field of ripe wheat.

The next day, he invited his girl friend to go with him on a ride in a small single-engined airplane, and she accepted. As they flew over the field, she noticed that large swatches had been cut in the wheat, spelling out LOLA, I LOVE YOU. WILL YOU MARRY ME?

What do you suppose Lola's response was?

* * *

The young farm girl's heart was won over, and she agreed to marry the persistent young man. Her future husband adopted a principle of asking that, if used correctly, can be hard to resist, Rule #6 (see Chapter 8). If you apply this rule in making your own requests, you can sometimes turn a certain "no" into a "yes."

Situation #7: Circular Request

Here is another letter I received:

Dear Mr. Ross,

My mother works very hard to raise my younger brother and me, and we both help her as much as we can.

I have been trying to find a job for over a year so I can help at home. Now that I'm 15, I can start a good-paying job for $3.35 an hour after school and on Saturdays.

My mom can't leave her work to drive me back and forth and my old bike keeps breaking down. The tires are shot. If you could please lend me money to buy a bike, I will pay you back $5 a week.

I'm going to work hard and become a millionaire like you.

M. N.
Dallas, Texas

If you were me, how would you answer?

* * *

I wrote back:

Dear M.,

I remember only too well how important a bike is to a 15-year-old. I was in a similar situation at your age, trying to help my family.

You can now start your job. Pick up your new Schwinn World 10-speed bike from Inwood Cycle Shop, 5627 W. Lovers Lane in Dallas.

Your wanting to help your family is all the repayment I need. I am interested in your financial progress, so write again.

From one millionaire to a future millionaire . . . keep pedaling.

This young man applied all ten of the rules of asking—and he did so masterfully.

His use of Rule #10 in particular, which I describe in Chapter 12, really made an impression on me. When you apply this principle, you automatically make the other person your ally and friend. He or she will bend over backward to help you; and even when help cannot be given, both of you will gain a great gift.

What are these ten rules of asking that I've referred to here? They are the principles that can increase your chances of success in every aspect of your life. To learn what they are and how to use them, just turn the page.

PART II

THE TEN RULES
OF ASKING

Chapter 3

Decide What You Need

Some of the people who read my syndicated column seem to think I'm the genie from Aladdin's lamp. They shower me with requests of every conceivable sort.

I'm happy to hear from such people, but unlike the genie, who promised to make any three wishes come true, I can promise nothing. In fact I say "yes" to only a small number of the many thousands of requests that come to me every month.

Why do I say "yes" to some, "no" to others? I don't act by whim, nor do I reach into a hat. The first thing I look for is a clear need, a purpose.

Perhaps the biggest reason so many people do not get what they want is that they are not clear about what it is that will make their lives better. They are really not sure what it is they want. The first, and most essential, rule of successful asking is this:

- Rule #1   **Know What You Really Need or Want.**

What if, when the genie offered Aladdin three wishes, Aladdin couldn't think of anything he really wanted? Or suppose Aladdin asked for three things he thought he wanted, but learned he didn't have much use for once he got them? What a waste of those magic wishes!

In our own lives, we make not three, but thousands of wishes. And there are genies who will help make those wishes come true: the people with whom we live, work, study, or socialize. They will gladly assist us toward our goals, if only we ask them. But first we've got to know what we want.

In my observation, it's often difficult for people to identify what they really need or want. But, I think, once they do, they will find many, many people who are willing to help them achieve their goals.

BE SURE OF WHAT YOU WANT BEFORE YOU MAKE A REQUEST

Certainty inspires confidence and support. If you are vague or uncertain in your request, other people will think twice about helping you out.

Let me give you an example from my "Thanks a Million" column:

Dear Mr. Ross,

I'm writing to ask if you would pay for the cost of helicopter flying lessons. They're offered at an airport close to me.

I just may want to make a career of piloting after I earn my license. I figure the lessons are approximately $100 an hour, with 40 hours needed to obtain a private license.

M. M.
Knoxville, Tennessee

My reply was a direct reaction to the writer's own lack of purpose:

Dear Miss M.,

I figure you're asking for $4,000 for something you *might* want to do. So now *you* figure out why I'm not mailing you a check.

Only approach others for help after you have formed a clear, definite idea of what you really need or want.

Never say:	"I might want to start a new business. Would you be interested in putting up some investment capital?"
Instead, say:	"I'm going to start a new business and need investment capital. Are you interested?"
Never say:	"I wish you kids would be more help around the house."
Instead, say:	"Jimmy and Jane, would you please start doing the dishes and taking out the garbage every night after dinner?"

Never say: "There doesn't seem to be much chance for advancement here, Mr. Brown. Are people ever promoted?"

Instead, say: "Mr. Brown, I'd like to move into systems engineering. If I come in on my own time to learn about it, would I be given a chance to switch jobs later on?"

Make sure you ask for something definite, something concrete. Notice the specifics in this letter:

Dear Mr. Ross,

I am 71 and live alone in a basement apartment. I never sleep well in this high-crime area of Brooklyn. I can't afford to move. Security is something we all worry about when we get to be my age. I'd feel a lot safer if I had steel bars on my windows. May I please have $300 for my seven basement windows before it's too late?

Mrs. L.O.
Brooklyn, New York

There isn't any doubt about what Mrs. O wants: $300 for bars to cover seven windows to make her feel safer. I sent the money plus my wishes for her safety and peace of mind. But what if she had merely written saying she felt unsafe in a high-crime area, and couldn't I help in some way? How could I say yes to that?

A Colorado man wrote me about his thirty-year-old brother. "He is a self-taught pianist, composer, screenwriter, and philosopher," the man said. "However, when it comes to earning a living, he has a hard time." The man asked if I could arrange for his brother to meet the "right" person to hear his music or read his work.

I wanted to help, but I was at a loss. "If there is a right person your brother would like to meet," I wrote, "let me know and I will try to arrange an interview."

It's hard for someone to help you if your request is too abstract or general. When approaching anyone for anything, try to communicate exactly what you want from them.

Avoid saying:	"I hope you can fix my car as soon as possible because I need it."
Instead, say:	"I need the car by five o'clock to go on a business trip. Could you please have it fixed by then?"
Avoid saying:	"Mom, could you lend me some money? I'll pay you back."
Instead, say:	"Mom, could you lend me $5 so I can go to the movies with Brian? I'll pay you back next Friday when I get my allowance."
Avoid saying:	"Hey, mister! You're blocking traffic."
Instead, say:	"Hey, mister! Would you move your truck ahead a few feet so we can get by?"

DON'T BE AFRAID TO ASK FOR THE MOON

In the summer of 1979 I toured the Blank Memorial Hospital for Children at Iowa Methodist Medical Center in Des Moines. While two employees of Baskin-Robbins ice cream served strawberry and vanilla cones, I handed out silver dollars and chatted with the kids.

A ten-year-old boy recovering from a tonsillectomy asked me if he too could become a millionaire someday. I explained, "Yes, you can, young man. Know what you want, work hard for what you want, keep dreaming, and don't give up."

At the end of the tour, a reporter from the *Des Moines Sunday Register* asked me why I put such big ideas into these children's minds. He explained that most of them were from poor families and their futures seemed pretty bleak. I replied, "I was born poorer than any child we met today in this hospital." I said, too, that people who scoff at wealth and make their children believe they can never be rich are misguided. "There's something wrong. They've given up hope. They use it as an excuse to say, 'It's impossible. I can't do it.'"

It is a tragedy of our times that so many people give up on themselves. If they let their dreams die, their hopes fade, their desires dwindle, then they certainly won't succeed. *Don't be afraid to think big!*

Too many people limit themselves by setting their goals too low. William Hazlitt, the English essayist, once said, "A strong passion for any object will ensure success, for the desire of the end will point out the means." If you know in your heart and soul what you want, you *can* succeed—and you can get others to help you. People will help you when they sense your desire.

In 1896, thirty-three-year-old Henry Ford passionately wanted to build something that had never been built before: a gasoline-driven horseless carriage. He didn't have much luck at first. Most people poured cold water on the idea, causing him to lose heart. What he desperately needed at that point was encouragement from someone who could appreciate his goal. So, at a convention, he approached a famous inventor and blurted out his dream. The inventor said, "A self-contained unit that carries its own fuel. That's the thing! Keep at it!"

Elated, Ford redoubled his efforts. Eventually, he formed the Ford Motor Company. The famous inventor who encouraged him was a man who had big dreams of his own—Thomas Edison.

Dare to desire. Don't be afraid of big, ambitious goals. Decide what you want, and stick to it. When I was eight, my mother scrubbed floors in exchange for violin lessons for me. I stuck it out for a year, but I had no musical talent or ambition. I did have financial ambitions, though; I wanted to become a millionaire. I kept that goal firmly in mind until at last I succeeded.

Your burning desire may not be for a million dollars. But a clear goal—and a clear idea of what you'll need to accomplish that goal—will go a long way toward making you successful. People will go out of their way to help you.

I got a letter from a young woman who made it easy for me to say yes. She told me exactly what she wanted, and precisely how I could help her get it. She wanted a career as an actress, and someday, an Oscar. She had talent, training, self-confidence and determination, but alas, no contacts. Could I introduce her to a good manager or agent?

I sensed a very strong desire in this young woman. I wrote back:

> Dear Miss M.,
>
> Everyone needs a break occasionally. This could be yours! I've arranged an interview and audition for you with a vice president at a top theatrical agency in Beverly Hills. He is in charge of TV casting and is looking for talent. Phone or write him immediately for an appointment. I always wanted to be thanked by somebody receiving their Oscar at the Academy Awards.

I don't care how old you are, or how unpromising your situation. You *can* claim or reclaim your dreams. But first you must decide what you need to accomplish your goal.

ASK FOR THE ESSENTIALS FIRST

Always start by asking for essentials, not extras. You'll get more support that way, and the extras—if you really need and want them—will follow.

A seventeen-year-old boy wrote me about his dream to own a $300,000 yacht. Of course I declined to help him. I did not doubt the boy's desire for a yacht, but what seventeen-year-old—or seventy-year-old for that matter—really *needs* a yacht?

Sometimes it's not so easy to tell genuine need from

simple desire. A Denver couple wrote me about a financial disaster. They had lost a considerable sum in the stock market. They asked me to replace their losses plus an amount equal to bank interest they would have earned.

I turned them down by saying, "You are the only people I know who charge interest in their request." It was clear to me that the couple didn't really "need" my check—they were merely brooding over the loss of their speculative investment.

Many people search for investment capital to start a new business, and get nowhere. This couple made the mistake of asking for a large sum that they really didn't need. One fellow wanted half a million dollars to hire a staff, set up impressive offices, and pay himself a comfortable salary. It might have been "nice" to start off that way, but potential investors raised their eyebrows in disapproval.

Plenty of other people have started successful businesses by asking friends, relatives, or bankers for a few hundred or thousand dollars for very specific needs. Elias Howe built the world's first sewing machine with just $500 borrowed from a friend. Steve Jobs and Steve Wosniac built their first few Apple computers with parts they got on credit from a local supplier.

The people who get on in this world are the ones who can work and live lean. They can make do with essentials; they don't demand extras. They ask for muscle; they don't ask for fat.

Too many people convince themselves they need fat; luxuries become "necessities" and wants become endless. Cut back your unrealistic wants and requests. You'll find that you'll be much more successful with the requests you do make. It pays to be selective in calling your shots.

DON'T ASK FOR THE WRONG THINGS

Sometimes people ask for things that will not help them get what they really want. Many years ago my friend Jeno Paulucci stood in a relief line waiting for a handout. "I couldn't stand it," he said later, "so I just stepped out of the line and never returned."

There's nothing wrong with asking for welfare or charity if you really need it, but Paulucci knew he could get along without it. He looked around for a way to earn some money. He thought he could make a business out of growing bean sprouts, and he asked a friend to lend him enough cash to get started. Years later, in 1966, he sold his Chun King Corporation for $63 million.

An Ontario woman once asked me for $30,000 so she could stop lying to her husband. Over several years, she had led him to think she was depositing more in their savings account than she actually was. She did it to keep him from being depressed about their lack of money. Now the lie had snowballed, and he thought they had $30,000 more than they actually did. She wrote, "In eighteen months our house mortgage comes due and he expects to pay it off with this money. I am desperate."

I could have gotten her out of this spot, but would that really have been best for her and her husband? Instead I wrote back, "I have read your letter many times. I've come to the conclusion you're not in the spot you think you are. Face your husband and tell him the situation as frankly as you told it to me in your letter. In no way could I help you perpetuate your lie. I'm not your last hope; the truth is."

Eric Hoffer, the longshoreman-philosopher, wrote: "Often the thing we pursue most passionately is but a substitute for the one thing we really want and cannot have." Too often we do pursue substitutes. Here's a perfect example:

Mary: "Let's go to the Bahamas. We had such a good time there on our honeymoon."

John: "We can't afford to go to the Bahamas. You know that."

Mary: "But we never have any time together anymore. You're always working."

John: "Do you think I like to work all the time? I'm trying to start a new business. Don't make it harder on me by talking about things we can't afford."

(A heated argument follows.)

Learn how to ask for what you *really* need or want, and you'll be more likely to get it. Let's replay the preceding scene:

Mary: "Remember our honeymoon, the good time we had together in the Bahamas?"

John: "Yeah."

Mary: "I wish we could spend some time together like that now. I really felt close to you then."

John: "We can't afford the Bahamas. And I can't afford the time. I'm trying to start a new business."

Mary: "I know. But how about a weekend
together? Somewhere nearby—it
doesn't have to be the Bahamas. I just
want us to be close again."

(They get together; that's what Mary really
wanted anyway.)

If you are economical in your requests, life will be
liberal in its response.

People often think they need certain things as a
prerequisite for other things. For example, a high
school junior in Detroit asked me to buy her a tape
recorder, an IBM electric typewriter, and an Apple
word processor so she could get started on a writing
career. I reminded her that Abraham Lincoln used a
pencil on the back of an envelope to write the Get-
tysburg Address.

A man I know asked his wife to make dinner a half
hour later every day, to give him time to jog. His wife
pointed out that a later dinner time would disrupt the
schedules of several other members of the family. The
fact is that her husband *could* find time to jog, even if
the dinner schedule stayed the same. When it comes
to performance, outside circumstances—though they
can make a difference—matter far less than internal
drive.

Don't let yourself believe you "need" a change in
outside circumstances to get what you want in life.
That kind of thinking is a trap. It can hold you back.

Ask for a change in circumstances only when you're
sure it will help; ask for it only when you are sure
you're not using your request as an excuse for inaction.

THE PERCY ROSS IMPROVEMENT PLAN FOR DECIDING WHAT YOU NEED

Remember, the world is full of genies waiting to grant your wishes. Be clear about what you need or want. Then turn to those around you—friends, family members, associates, influential strangers. You'll almost certainly find someone to help you along your way.

To clarify your goals, try following these two suggestions:

1. Focus on a real need during the next few days. Strive in some way to fulfill that need every day for the next month. Tell yourself you *can* and *should* have it met.

2. Ask someone for something related to that need. Do it tomorrow or within a few days. Keep on asking for something that will help you arrive at your goal in the weeks and months ahead. For example, if you want to start a business, ask a friend or relative for help: "Aunt Hannah, I want to start a day-care center. I think I can really help young kids, and I think I would be making more of a contribution doing that than staying in my typing job. . . . I need advice. Where can I find a place to rent? How can I get a bank loan? Will you help me?"

The world is yours. Pick your mountain and start your climb. There are plenty of people who will gladly give you a hand.

Chapter 4

Find the Right Ear

Some people have a knack for pulling a rabbit out of a hat. One such person was Norman Bel Geddes. At the age of twenty-four, he was nearly broke and out of work. He didn't know how he was going to support his wife and young daughter.

One day, with just $5.83 in his pocket, he sat down on a park bench and noticed a magazine lying next to him. He picked it up and flipped through the pages. One of the articles caught his eye. In it, a prominent banker, Otto Kahn, was quoted as saying, "Millionaires should help artists."

Bel Geddes stood up, excited. He rushed to a Western Union office and spent a good part of his $5.83 on a telegram to Kahn, asking for money. He explained his situation and his desire to produce plays and design sets. The next day, Kahn wired Bel Geddes $400.

With this stake—and Kahn's vote of confidence— Bel Geddes went to New York and got a job designing opera sets. He went on to become one of Broadway's best producers. He also earned an international reputation as a designer of auto bodies, chairs, refrigerators, and other consumer items.

Bel Geddes took a long shot—and it worked. But he also correctly applied the second rule of asking:

- **Rule #2   Ask the Right Person.**

Otto Kahn had the means and the desire to help artists. That's what Bel Geddes figured, and he was right.

Whether you're asking for money, for a date, for directions, or simple advice, it's important to ask the right person. Here is an example of what can happen when someone does not ask for help from the right person:

A radiator broke in a room above a public library in a small New Jersey town. Water began pouring through the library ceiling onto the books, flooding the floor. It was Halloween evening, and the place was empty except for a lone librarian. She called the police and the fire department, but nobody came to help. Many books were damaged.

The next day, town officials investigated. The police sergeant who received the call explained, "She asked for mops. We don't normally send police cars when people ask for mops. If you have a broken pipe, you call a plumber. If she would have asked for police assistance, we would have sent someone."

Instead, the sergeant gave her the phone number of the fire department. They didn't have any mops either, and so she hung up.

Personally, I think the police sergeant and whoever answered the fire department phone could have been more helpful. But the librarian could have made her request much clearer too. First, she violated Rule #1, "Know what you really need." She asked for mops; what she really needed was help in coping with a flood.

The librarian also violated Rule #2: "Ask the right person." The police were not the right people to help with this particular problem. A plumber or the fire department would have been better equipped to stop the leak and clean up the water. She did call the fire department, but she did not make a point of talking to the right person there. She simply accepted what the person who answered the phone said, and then hung up. Instead, she might have done as follows:

Fireman: We don't have any mops.

Librarian: The police said you could help me. We've got a flood here.

Fireman: Lady, what can I say? We don't have any mops.

Librarian: Who is this? Are you the fire chief?

Fireman: No, I'm one of the volunteers.

Librarian: May I speak with the chief, please?

Fireman: He's out behind the town hall, helping to judge the Halloween contest.

Librarian: This is an emergency. We've got a lot of valuable books here that belong to the town. They could be ruined. They're worth thousands of dollars.

Fireman: Hold on. I'll get the chief.

If you want to get what you need, contact the right person. The right person is someone with the *means* and the *desire* to help.

ASK SOMEONE WHO CAN—AND WANTS—TO SAY YES

No matter what you're after—assistance, a gift, a loan, a favor, a job—approach someone who has the *power* and the *motivation* to give it to you. Successful salespeople apply this principle instinctively. Before spending time with customers, they ask themselves:

- "Do they want what I'm selling?"
- "Do they have the money to buy?"

If the answer to either question is "no," the salesperson looks for other prospects.

No matter what kind of "yes" you're after, if you ask the right people, you'll get more yeses.

Let me give you an example of the wrong person to ask. A man wrote me in care of my syndicated newspaper column, "Thanks a Million." Like the request from Norman Bel Geddes, this one also had to do with art:

Dear Percy,

All my life I have admired art and could only afford a few inexpensive paintings. At the age of 73, now I would like at least one master. I think you can buy one from $200,000 up. Could you handle such a request?

K. M.
Toronto, Ontario

You can probably guess my response. I wrote back:

Dear Mr. M,

Could I? . . . Yes! Will I? . . . No!

I had the means but not the desire to help. I prefer to help people who, like Norman Bel Geddes, really need help, and who also show a willingness to help themselves. Again, look for someone with both the *power* and the *motivation* to give you what you want.

Many years ago, Dick Samson wanted a job as a data-processing systems engineer with IBM. He went to IBM's corporate employment office in New York City. He had just received a B.A. in English from Whittier College, California. He was told that the only positions open for him were in technical writing.

Dick wasn't interested in a technical writing job. So he went to a private employment agency and told them he wanted a job in systems engineering "with any company except IBM."

The employment counselor asked him, "Why not IBM?"

"Because I went to IBM's corporate employment office on Madison Avenue, and they said all they've got are jobs in technical writing."

The counselor smiled and said, "You've come to the right place." He arranged an interview for Dick at a downtown Manhattan office of IBM, and within a week Dick was employed there as a trainee in data-processing systems engineering.

The people in IBM's corporate employment office had the means to place Dick in the job he had asked for. But apparently they didn't have the motivation;

they wanted to fill a technical writing spot. The private employment counselor had the motivation as well as the means for getting Dick what he wanted.

Often the right person to approach is the one who has a certain skill or special knowledge. A few years ago a Pennsylvania man in the strip-mining business received notification from Washington that he had to restore the land he had stripped. Restoration was no simple matter because of the destroyed topsoil and a residue of sulfuric acid. Little would grow in the rocky, sour land. Who could help him solve the problem?

He turned to his brother-in-law, an advertising man named William "Turk" Jones. "Turk," he said, "you majored in biology. Anybody knows you can't grow anything in coal-mine spoils, but the law says we have to try."

Jones turned out to be the right person to ask. Not only did he know something about plants, but his advertising experience had taught him to turn drawbacks into advantages. "If customers say your shampoo leaves their hair oily," he said, "you turn it around and sell it to people with dry-scalp problems."

Thinking about the stripped land, Jones tried to figure out a way to turn the minuses into pluses. "If you set out seedlings in grass or underbrush, the surrounding plants choke them. But on a rock pile there is no competition for light or moisture. And you don't have to plow. The stripping has loosened the earth and rock down to 50 feet."

There still remained the problem of acid-contaminated soil. He began researching varieties of trees, and found a European white birch that had an unusual tolerance for soil acidity. Soon the stripped land was green with healthy trees. Jones then found other strip-mine operators who were interested in restoration, and built himself a thriving new business.

The moral of this story: Find out who is best qualified to give you what you need, and approach that person.

DON'T BE AFRAID TO APPROACH SUCCESSFUL PEOPLE

In many cases the best person to ask is someone who has power, position, or authority: the head of a bank, the president of a company, an elected official, or some other prominent citizen. Do not hesitate to approach such people if your need is genuine. They have the power to help because of their position, their contacts, their wealth, and the information at their fingertips. And I have often found they have the motivation to help too. You see, they got where they are because they received help from others. They've been through it all; they know what it's like to come up in the world. Believe me, they've often got a lot of empathy for others who are trying to make their way too. Approach them. Explain what you're after. You may have a better chance of getting a "yes" from them than from anyone else.

I have approached many bank presidents in my time. I got a $30,000 business loan when my net worth was a fraction of that. Later, I got enough money to carry on my polyethylene plastic business when it was half a million dollars in debt. So if it

FIND THE RIGHT EAR

makes sense to do so, speak to top people, and put your proposition to them.

When I came up with the idea for my newspaper column, I submitted it to over a dozen prominent newspaper syndicates. They all turned me down. I was disappointed and confused. What was I doing wrong? Was I approaching the syndicates properly? I needed some information and guidance.

I decided to approach Charles W. Bailey, editor of the *Minneapolis Tribune*. He didn't know me, but I thought he might help me. Over the phone, I told him about my column idea and the trouble I was having. "If you could give me a few minutes of your time," I said, "I certainly would appreciate it." He agreed to see me and I went to his office.

Mr. Bailey said he liked my idea, and offered to write a letter to Dennis Allen, president of the Register and Tribune Syndicate (now part of King Features) in Des Moines. Bailey's letter opened the door. If I hadn't gone to Bailey, I might not be a columnist today.

Bailey was the right person to approach for two reasons. First, he knew Dennis Allen and had some influence with him. Second—and more important— he put his finger on why the syndicates were turning me down. They were suspicious of me; they doubted my means, and they worried about my motives. Bailey, in his letter to Allen, dispelled those suspicions:

Dear Dennis,

A local millionaire named Percy Ross—whom you may have read of or seen giving away silver dollars or performing other philanthropic functions—came in today with an idea for a syndicated column.

Because of the publicity he receives, he gets a lot of mail—maybe 500 to 1,000 letters a week—much of it from people who ask for money. He sends money, generally in modest amounts but occasionally in spectacular sums, to some of those who ask for it.

He thinks the appeals and his responses, including his donations, would make a syndicated column. It seems to me that it might go—sort of an Ann Landers who offers not only advice but help in a more concrete way.

In any event, I took the liberty of suggesting to him that he might contact you and try to interest you in the idea. I'd be glad to discuss it with you if you want to give me a call.

Mr. Ross's means are substantial, his sources of income are solid, and his motives uncomplicated, in my view. At the least you would be intrigued to talk to him, I think.

Sincerely,
Chuck Bailey

At Bailey's urging, Dennis Allen said he would look over many sample columns if I would send them. He wasn't sold on the columns I submitted, but he didn't turn me away either. He worked with me to help create a more professional format and style, then said he would give the column a try. In less than a year, seventy-five newspapers had signed up.

APPROACH AN INTERMEDIARY

If the "right person" is prominent or successful, you may not be able to approach him or her directly. There will be a gatekeeper, usually a secretary. You are no doubt familiar with the barriers this person puts up:

- "He's in a meeting."
- "She's very busy today."
- "Could you tell me why you want to talk with him?"
- "She's not available. Why don't you write her a letter."

Most people regard secretaries as enemies, alligators in a moat designed to keep everyone from approaching the king in the castle. And too many people treat secretaries with condescension, with the result that secretaries do not go out of their way to help them. But my longtime secretary, Nancy Webber, will tell you that any secretary can be your ally, a friendly gatekeeper who lowers the drawbridge and ushers you in.

When approaching a prominent or successful person, I always start by asking for the secretary. Here is a typical conversation:

> *Percy Ross:* Hello, could you tell me the name of Mr. Johnson's secretary, please?
>
> *Receptionist:* Marilyn Baker.
>
> *Percy Ross:* Thank you. May I speak with her, please?

Secretary:	Mr. Johnson's office.
Percy Ross:	Hello, this is Percy Ross calling from Minneapolis. Are you Marilyn Baker?
Secretary:	Yes.
Percy Ross:	I wonder if you could help me, Ms. Baker. I'd like to talk to Mr. Johnson about an investment. It would take five minutes of his time on the telephone . . .
Secretary:	What kind of an investment? Are you selling stocks or bonds?
Percy Ross:	No. I own a folding-carton company. I'm looking for investment capital. I know Mr. Johnson sometimes invests in established businesses, and I think he might be interested in this opportunity. If you could possibly arrange for me to talk to him for five minutes, I sure would appreciate it. In five minutes, I could give him enough details for him to decide if he's interested. Could you possibly set up a time for me?
Secretary:	I'll see what I can do, Mr. Ross.

I have found that secretaries like Nancy are very important people. They practically run the place. They are *the* individuals to approach *first* whenever you want to ask for anything from a key man or woman. If you ask for secretaries by name and explain your purpose to them, you flatter them and get them on your side. You also help them do their job—which is to protect the boss's time while bringing matters of real concern to his or her attention.

There is another reason secretaries are the right people to approach first: Trusted secretaries can be much more convincing to a boss than someone unknown who is calling in. They are in a position to say to the boss, "I think it might be smart to talk to this person."

I always bring secretaries into my confidence and make them feel they are doing me, as well as their boss, a favor. They very seldom turn me down.

Secretaries aren't the only intermediaries you should approach. Coworkers, friends, or business associates can also pave the way to an important person. I have found that if I can involve a business person's spouse in a project, it becomes a lot easier to involve the business person.

Sometimes the best intermediary is a person who ranks *above*, rather than below, the individual who can help you. Often I arrange appointments at banks for people who need loans. First I call the president of a local bank and ask, "Which of your loan officers would be the best one to consider helping this person?" The president knows the right officer, and he can get the ball rolling in a favorable way.

ASK THE APPROPRIATE PERSON

When help is needed, there is always an appropriate person to ask. Think about who that person is. If you need money, perhaps a relative is the right person to approach; or a potential investor; or a banker. It all depends on the circumstances.

A young man in the South wanted to go into business for himself. His dream was to set up a foundry, but he didn't know how to get started. Who could help him? It took awhile for the obvious person to come to mind. His own father—an engineer who lived in California—had worked in a small enterprising company for years, and knew several successful business people.

Many long-distance phone calls ensued, and the two of them developed a rich new relationship. The young man's foundry was established and it became successful.

KEEP LOOKING UNTIL YOU FIND THE RIGHT PERSON

Sometimes, as with the young man above, careful thought or intuition will lead you to the right person. At other times, as with Norman Bel Geddes, you must trust to luck.

If you cannot immediately locate the right person to ask for what you need, ask several people who are in the "ball park," and keep asking until you connect. A New Jersey couple wanted to do some home repairs and install a new kitchen. After talking with local contractors specializing in kitchens, they quickly became discouraged. The estimates ran from $28,000 upward for the kitchen alone—much more than they could afford. The repairs would add a minimum of $10,000 to that amount.

They checked with contractors in nearby towns, and told their friends of their need. Finally, through a friend who was a commercial artist, they met a retired high school teacher who ran a store specializing in fine wood furniture and cabinetry. He wanted to get into the remodeling business, and offered to put in the kitchen and do the repairs for a total cost of $25,000, including appliances.

The couple was overjoyed, and the construction worked out very well.

Have faith. The people who can help you—the ones with the means and the desire—exist somewhere. They're out there. Look, and keep looking. Eventually they will turn up.

THE PERCY ROSS IMPROVEMENT PLAN FOR FINDING THE RIGHT EAR

If you want to improve your ability to approach the right person, first apply Rule #1: Know what you really need. Then do the following:

1. List people who might say "yes." Do it for each need or request you have. Suppose you need advice on getting a new job, help with a personal problem, or a means of earning additional income. Ask yourself:

- Who has what I need?
- Who has enough to give?
- Who would like to help a person like me?
- Who has the necessary skill or knowledge to help me?

61

- What intermediary person could help me approach the right person?
- Is there an obvious "correct" person I'm overlooking?

2. Mentally rehearse asking the right people. Imagine calling the person on the phone or talking to the person face-to-face. Mentally, or out loud before a mirror, state your situation, and ask for what you need.

If you are shy or nervous, rehearsing will help you develop the courage to make your request.

3. Ask someone for something. Pick a need and a "right person." Then ask that person for what you need. Do it tomorrow or within the next few days.

If you are hesitant to ask for what you want, pick something very small or relatively insignificant at first: a favor, the loan of a tool, a suggestion. If you approach the right person, you have a good chance of getting what you ask for. Your success will breed enthusiasm, and your enthusiasm will breed more success.

Remember, asking for what you want is a good thing to do. It helps you reach your goals. And it often gives you the wherewithal to help others as well as yourself.

Chapter 5

Your Best Foot Forward

When you approach someone for a favor, an investment, or any type of help or cooperation, don't just blurt out your request; first think about your approach. Always put your request in the best possible light. To be as influential as possible, always apply this important rule:

- **Rule #3   Prepare a Good Case.**

Once you've decided what it is you really want or need (Rule #1), and you've picked the right person to ask (Rule #2), you must decide *how* to ask—how to put the best possible face on your request.

Do you know which of your two profiles is most photogenic? Actors and actresses know, and they insist, whenever possible, on being photographed with their more photogenic side toward the camera. When asking for anything—a favor, money, assistance, cooperation—you too should take care to feature your best "profile."

PUT YOUR BEST FOOT FORWARD

Imagine yourself in this situation: You are running for the U.S. Congress against a man who served as a general in the army. You were in the army too, but did not rise above private. The two of you appear together in a debate before the voters. The general politely refers to the wide difference between your ranks, pointing to his great experience as a planner, policy maker, and coordinator. Obviously, he is better qualified for the many responsibilities of the office.

Now it is your turn to speak. Your challenge is to convince the listeners to give you their votes. What is the best "foot" you can put forward?

Here is how Private John Allen appealed to voters in 1885 when debating General William F. Tucker. He said, "I admit I was only a private. In fact, I was just a picket who stood guard over the general when he slept. And now, all you fellows who were generals and had privates standing guard over you, you vote for General Tucker. All you boys who were privates and stood guard over the generals, you vote for Private John Allen." Allen won the election and served in Congress for sixteen years.

The moral here is to always put your best foot forward. If you do, you may get a "yes" even when a "no" seems inevitable.

Before asking anyone for anything, do your homework. Consider the merits of your situation, and plan how to get those merits across. Cover all your bases by preparing the very best case you can.

EXPLAIN WHY YOU NEED ASSISTANCE

People will usually hesitate to help if they feel you are capable of getting what you want without them. Therefore a key part of any effective request is to show that you really need the help of the person you're asking.

When the Chrysler Corporation was in danger of going out of business, Lee Iacocca asked and got the federal government to guarantee massive loans. Iacocca convinced officials that the jobs Chrysler provided were vital to the economy, but this point alone was not enough to win a "yes." Iacocca also had to show that Chrysler could not get the necessary funds any other way—and he did.

Let me give you a more down-to-earth example of what I mean. Recently two sixteen-year-old boys each asked me for $100. One got a "yes"; the other didn't. Notice how their letters differ:

Dear Mr. Ross,

I'm a 16-year-old boy with big ambitions to become a professional skateboarder. Although skateboarding is considered by many to be a menace to society, it is a legitimate sport.

Like all sports, it has its dangers. That's why I'm seeking your help. My mom wants me to wear safety equipment. I would, but I don't have any. If you could possibly send $100 to cover the cost, I would be extremely grateful.

R. K.
Dayton, Ohio

Dear Mr. Ross,

I enjoy creating my own comics with characters I myself make up. Now I have the opportunity to start a small comic book business, with the help of a few friends. I have made arrangements with a local store to sell the books and have planned for the necessary copies, employment, and scheduling.

The problem is I do not have the money to cover all the costs of starting such a company. I'm only 16. Could you please send $100 to help with the opening costs? I've included a sample of my work to help you decide whether or not my business deserves a chance.

M. P. B.
Johnstown, Pennsylvania

The second boy got my "yes"—with a check for $200, not $100—because he not only convinced me of his talent and determination but that he had thoroughly tapped his own resources and really did need a hand. To the first boy I wrote, "Is there any reason why you can't earn this money yourself?"

If you want a yes, convince the other person that *their* consent, help, or cooperation is important, if not essential. For example:

Less effective:	"Julie, would you handle my calls for a few minutes?" ("I guess I can, but I've got work of my own, you know.")
More effective:	"Julie, Mr. Sommers wants me in his office and Bob is out sick. Would you mind handling my calls for a few minutes?" ("No problem.")
Less effective:	"Jim, we'd like you to run for the school board." ("I'm too busy in my new job.")
More effective:	"Jim, you're the only one we know who can cut a budget without destroying morale or performance. We'd like you to run for the school board." ("Well . . .")

SHOW THAT THE PERSON'S HELP WILL MAKE A DIFFERENCE

When Lee Iacocca asked for federal assistance, he had to do more than demonstrate the need for loan guarantees. He also had to demonstrate that the guarantees would be effective in helping Chrysler succeed. If the odds were that Chrysler would fold anyway, in spite of the help, then why should the government pour good money down the drain?

All people, like federal officials, hate to see cash go to waste, especially their own. They also hate to waste valuable time, effort, or skill. So when you ask people for assistance, give some evidence that it will make a real difference.

When my business, Poly-Tech, was about to go into bankruptcy, none of the New York lending institutions would give me the funds I needed to continue in business and recover from its half-million-dollar debt. I went back to Minneapolis and banged on the doors of every bank and secondary lending institution around. All I got was a string of "no's." Finally there was a spark of interest from Kenneth Rahn, president of Northern Finance Company. He and Northern's board chairman, Gene Hanson, agreed to visit my plant and consider a loan.

The chances of a "yes" from any lending institution were very small because Poly-Tech was already in Chapter 11 of the U.S. Bankruptcy law. That meant we were under the jurisdiction of the court, and the rights of any new lender would be secondary. Secured creditors—those to whom I owed the $500,000—had first crack at our assets. Normally, in bankruptcy proceedings, creditors prefer that the firm be liquidated so they can get at least a portion of the money owed them. If Northern were to lend us money at this point, and Poly-Tech were to be sold, Northern would get its money back only *after* primary creditors got paid off. The chances of Poly-Tech being sold for more than $500,000 were nil.

Another complicating factor was that Northern could not make loans unless it was in a first-security position. Therefore, in order for Northern to lend us any money, two things had to happen. First, our creditors had to relinquish their primary position to Northern. Second, Northern, as well as our creditors, had to believe we could come out of debt and succeed. Otherwise the creditors had the chance of accepting about 10 cents on the dollar.

I knew that I had to prepare a good case for myself. I did my best. Here are some of the things I did to prepare my case:

- I made a private pledge to myself to repay all my creditors 100 percent on the dollar, something very unusual in bankruptcy proceedings.
- I told Mr. Rahn and Mr. Hanson that in my opinion our product had a great future. I did my best to convince the bankers that polyethylene film plastic would be one of great products of this century. Rahn and Hanson showed interest.
- Before Rahn and Hanson visited our plant, I made sure everything was ship-shape. There wasn't a smudge of grease on a machine, not a bit of scrap on the floor; everything was neat, clean, and orderly. I made sure the parking lot was spotless. I even asked my employees to wear clean shirts and to be freshly shaved.
- Since business was slow, I shut down production for two days before their visit. Then, when Rahn and Hanson walked through the door, we were geared up and running at full production.
- I gave them the best plant tour you can imagine. Everything I did gave the impression that Poly-Tech was a company that could and would succeed.

Later Rahn told me, "I was convinced that you had business acumen, honesty, and determination to succeed. All you needed was money." He also told me he had visited the company years earlier, before I bought it. "I saw it when it was just a scrap heap." During the present tour, he saw the potential for a financially successful business.

I had a provisional okay! Now just one obstacle stood in the way. Before Northern could give us a dime, our creditors had to give Northern the first-security position. I talked to the creditors; so did an attorney; so did representatives of Northern. I needed a majority of votes. One by one, the creditors agreed.

Northern lent us the money we needed. Within three years, Poly-Tech paid all creditors in full plus interest. And three years after that, we sold the company for $8 million.

In my experience, it really pays to prepare a good case for yourself. We all stand blind to the future, and our prospects may seem dark and bleak. But if we communicate our needs, hopes, and desires to others, we may see the bloom of bright new possibilities.

Suppose someone asked *you* to help them raise money to prospect for gold in the desert. You'd probably laugh. But only a year ago I helped just such an Arizona woman who had gold dust in her eyes. You see, she made a good case for herself; she convinced me her plans to dig for gold might pan out:

Dear Mr. Ross,

Really need your help. I've been a lady prospector for eight years and have found some very good veins of precious metal. Have quite a few claims legally recorded and ready for more work.

I've spent all the money I have for assays and assessment work—down to my last $25. I'm an eternal optimist (as all prospectors have to be) and know there is that pay lode just down there, not too far, but must drill and dig.

I don't have the prospector's donkey, but do have a Jeep Cherokee. Can I interest you in helping me with a loan?

R. M. C.
Pearce, Arizona

This woman's record of past success indicated that she knew her business and just might succeed. It was because of the second and third sentences in her letter that I took her request seriously. I wrote back:

Dear Mrs. C.

Yes, I'm interested in helping. I phoned Vic Howard, vice president of the Interstate Bank of Arizona in Tucson. Bring a list of your assets, liabilities, and plans. Mr. Howard will talk with you about a loan.

No matter what you want from others, show them you can succeed with their help. You'll get more support if you do.

- If you're running for office, convince people that if they give you their votes you can win.
- If you want advice from a busy person, explain how the information you need will help you solve a problem or get ahead.
- If you're applying for a job, convince the interviewer you can do well at the job if he or she hires you.

- If you want more responsibility in your present job, demonstrate that you can rise to the challenge.
- If you're looking for investors in a new business, show that the business can prosper.

Don't just *say* you can run with the ball if the person gives it to you. Offer *evidence:* facts, figures, expert opinions.

If what you want is more abstract or emotional, again show that someone's help can make a difference. For example, if you need encouragement when you're down, let the other person know that his or her support might lift your spirits. "I'm too uptight. I'm afraid I'll blow the interview. Will you help me relax?"

A GOOD CASE SPEAKS FOR ITSELF

To make a good case for yourself, (1) put your best foot forward, (2) state clearly and specifically what you need, (3) explain why you need it, and (4) show how the person's help will make a difference. If you cover all the bases—prepare your case with all these four points in mind—your request will be much more convincing.

Here is a request for help from a would-be model. How well do you think the writer did in making her request?

Dear Mr. Ross,

Ever since I was little, I always wanted to be a fashion model. I am 5 feet 8 inches, 128 lbs.

(must lose 10), blessed with nice legs and a nice figure. I've done some modeling locally and friends tell me I am attractive and photogenic.

I've made many, many sacrifices and denied myself luxuries to save $300 toward a trip to New York, where I hope to be interviewed for a career in modeling.

Can you possibly arrange an interview for me at the Wilhelmina Agency or the Ford Modeling Agency? I would appreciate a definite appointment because I don't know when I will ever be able to save enough to go there again.

I want a good future for myself, Mr. Ross. Will you please help me get started?

H. L.
Chicago, Illinois

I liked the young woman after reading her letter, and I wanted to help her. She did a fairly good job of putting her best foot forward. She painted a positive picture of her abilities and her desires. She covered Rule #1 (know what you really need or want) quite well. She stated specifically what kind of help she wanted: an introduction and definite appointment with one of two modeling agencies, which she named.

She didn't do especially well in explaining *why* she needed what she asked for. Nor did she explain why she needed it from *me*. Couldn't she arrange appointments for herself?

But she showed quite clearly how the help would make a difference. She said that a definite appointment would be very helpful since lack of funds would prevent her from making another trip; and she indicated that my help might pave the way to a good future.

Overall, her request was a winner because of its clarity, concreteness, and relative completeness. I telephoned the Wilhelmina Agency in New York and spoke with the president, William Weinberg. He offered to review the woman's snapshots and to interview her should he like what he saw. I told Miss L. that I would pay for her round-trip expenses to the Big Apple.

Cover all the bases, as best you can, when preparing your case. It will make quite a difference in the answer you get. Here's a letter from a woman who did just that:

Dear Mr. Ross,

My story: My marriage at 16 lasted only two weeks. My son Tim was born nine months later. For six years I've worked three different jobs at a time, twelve hours a day, in order to make ends meet. I could never get a decent job because of my dyslexia. It wasn't easy but I stayed out of debt. No welfare for us!

Four years ago, when Tim started school, I started my own business called Mid-West Rags. From my total savings of $150, I bought a battered, rundown '71 Toyota pickup truck that I learned to fix myself. I went to Goodwill Industries with my last few dollars and bought a 500-lb. bale of used unwanted clothing. This is how I got started in the rag business.

I cut, sort, wash, and pack all of the different kinds of cloth. Tim helps me after school. I sell the cotton for industrial wiping rags, the wool I sell to mills for recycling. I have also developed a profitable market for all of the other materials—down to the very last button.

Now for the sad part. At 27, just as my business got going and I thought I could hire some part-time help, my world crashed! My truck died! Now I can't pick up and deliver my rags. I'm desperate. I will lose all my business unless you can help me get a dependable used truck. Please answer this letter even if you can't help me. Somehow my son and I will make it, but we could use some help. We will not go on welfare!

Ms. P. G.
St. Paul, Minnesota

I wrote back:

Dear Ms. G.,

I'm impressed! I can also appreciate your initiative. I'll meet you half-way. Find a good used truck that will best suit your purpose, and I will contribute one-half of the cost . . . if you arrange to finance the other half.

Well, it didn't take her long. She found a nice, clean, used '80 Nissan for $4,000, and I sent her my check.

Ms. G. covered all four parts of Rule #3 (prepare a good case) in her letter: (1) She put her best foot forward by telling about her positive qualities and her desire to build a good future for herself and her young son; (2) She stated very clearly what she wanted: help in getting a dependable truck; (3) She told me why she needed it: to continue picking up and delivering rags, her source of livelihood. She also said why she approached me; she was desperate, having no money of her own; (4) She indicated the difference my help would make; it would keep her self-sufficient, allow her to maintain her pride, and keep her off welfare. With this kind of airtight case, how could I refuse her?

THE PERCY ROSS IMPROVEMENT PLAN FOR PUTTING YOUR BEST FOOT FORWARD

To get better at preparing a good case (Rule #3), try the following:

1. Jot down a few things you plan to ask people for. On a piece of paper, list things you want from others: a raise, a promotion, an <u>interview</u>, help around the house, forgiveness, a bank loan. Include everything from asking a customer for new business leads, to asking your employees for ideas.

2. Prepare a good case for at least one of those requests. Pick an item from your list. Then consider these questions:

- *"How can I put my best foot forward?"*
  Rehearse asking for the item on your list. Keep imagining different approaches until you find a positive, upbeat, convincing presentation. For example, as a boy I had the job of collecting money from my father's delinquent creditors. After re-

viewing various possibilities in my mind, I decided my best approach would be to ask sincerely for the money owed—not to show disapproval when people said they couldn't pay—and to gratefully accept any partial payment, however small.

- *"What, exactly, do I want?"*

  Be as concrete as you can about amounts, numbers, dates, and other specifics. If you are going to ask for a loan, be prepared to say how much you want, when and why you need it, and when and how you plan to repay it.

- *"Why do I need it?"*

  Ask yourself why you cannot provide the item for yourself, and why the person you plan to ask can best help you. If you plan to ask a friend or co-worker for a favor, you might explain, "I can't do it myself because I'll be out of town, and you're the only one besides me who knows how to do it right."

- *"What difference will this person's help make?"*

  Ask yourself how the help you have requested will bring about the change you want. For example, if you plan to ask a supplier to speed up a delivery of materials, tell him why you must have delivery quickly. "If you can get it to us by Friday, we'll be able to complete a job and make the delivery to Apex on time. It's a trial order, and if Apex likes our service, they're going to place some very big orders with us."

3. *Ask for something in the next few days.* If you present a well-prepared case, the chances are you'll get a "yes" for your efforts.

Make it a habit to prepare a strong case when asking for anything, little or big. Never forget to apply Rule #3. You'll find you'll get a lot more of what you ask for.

Chapter 6

Prime the Pump

If you've ever lived in the country, you've probably used an old-fashioned hand-operated pump. You know that such a pump often stops cooperating and stubbornly refuses to draw water. In that situation, you've got to coax it back into service by pouring in a little water, to help it develop suction. Then it becomes your true friend again, gushing forth all the water you need. The same principle applies to asking. Sometimes you have to prime other people with a little giving of your own; then watch them respond with a "yes" to your request.

A good way to persuade people to do anything is to apply the fourth rule of asking:

- **Rule #4   Give in Order to Receive.**

The Bible says, "Give, and it shall be given unto you; good measure . . . and running over, shall men give into your bosom." I've found that if you give what you can, you'll get more than you need.

During the Christmas holidays of 1980, I found a way to partially repay the Salvation Army for the help they gave my family when I was a boy. I stood at their kettle in Rockefeller Center in New York City, and encouraged passersby to make contributions.

I raised a lot of money that day by using a very effective method. I offered a silver dollar to each person who made a contribution, however small. Most people dropped more than a dollar into the kettle, and the drive was a great success.

When you ask for something, you don't have to give dollars in return as I did. But you must give *something*: respect, appreciation, pride, human warmth, or the prospect of future success. Equally important, you must show that you are a giving person—someone worthy of help and support.

GIVE SOMETHING TO THE GIVER

One question you should keep in mind, whether you ask someone for money, cooperation, or a favor, is this: Why should they say yes? In other words, what's in it for them?

When I sold eggs door-to-door as a boy, my father urged me to give my customers a thirteenth egg with the dozen every so often. My father's advice stood me in good stead: It really helped build repeat business.

Later, when I needed a raise to get married, I got the raise by giving something tangible to my employers: extra effort and extra profits. I was working for the Duluth Hide & Fur Company at the time, making

$75 a month. I needed $100 a month. Before asking for the raise, I decided to make a good impression. I wanted to create a positive climate for my request.

I went on the road on a Monday, planning to come back as usual on Friday. I concentrated on bringing back the most profitable truckload of hides and fur pelts I possibly could. If hides were 7 cents a pound, I would try to buy them for 6¾ cents. I did everything I could to make those purchases at the lowest possible price.

I told the hide dealers I bought from about my situation. "When I get home, I'm going to ask for a raise so that I can get married. I want to make sure I don't overpay you. If you wouldn't mind helping me, maybe some time in the future I can help you." I had no problem buying cattle hides at market value—and some even at a little bit less. The situation was the same with the raw fur pelts I was buying. I not only brought home a good load of hides, but also 650 mink pelts, 1,300 weasels, and about 4,500 muskrats.

I had bought everything that week that I knew was going to average below market price. I came home on Friday and put everything in the company garage. Saturday morning Mr. Davis and Mr. Beck, the two partners, met me while the truck was being unloaded. They didn't know the cost yet, of course. We took all the furs upstairs and graded them for size and quality. Mr. Beck said, "These are not bad furs, Percy." They were probably thinking these pelts were going to cost them a bundle. I arranged all the pelts on the floor upstairs, putting the nicest-looking ones on top. I wanted everything to look like money in the bank.

And then Mr. Beck said, "Have you got the purchase invoices?" As I went downstairs to get them, I wondered whether I should wait until Sunday morning to ask for my raise. That was when everything would normally be added up. "No," I said to myself, "I'll do it *now*."

I went back upstairs and handed him the invoices and said, "Mr. Beck, there's something on my mind. I need to earn $25 more a month. I'm going to be getting married soon and I don't make enough to support a wife."

He said, "No. Not a chance."

"Well," I replied, "I may have to look for a different kind of work." Notice I didn't say a *better job*; I said a *different kind of work*. I knew I could get a job with any of their competitors, but I didn't want to shove my request down their throat.

And so there I was with a "no"; but my employers hadn't yet added up the invoices I'd handed them. I left, and took my time getting home. I was pretty sure they would take the weights and tally up the costs right away. They were always eager to figure how much money they could make on a load. If I overpaid, they would certainly reprimand me. When I arrived at my fiancée's home for dinner, she said, "Honey, there's a telephone call for you from Mr. Beck, and he wants to see you tomorrow morning."

The next morning I met with Mr. Beck and Mr. Davis in their office. They didn't say a thing about the merchandise I brought in, but Mr. Beck said, "You know, we've been thinking. You've been here a couple of years, and you've been doing a pretty good job. Mr. Davis and I think you've earned the $25 raise you asked for."

And that's how I got my first raise. Soon they were sending me all over the country to buy from the biggest dealers. Within several years, they put me in charge of a separate hide and fur dealership. They doubled my salary, in addition to giving me half the profits. I was on the way to making my first fortune.

The point here is to think of the other person's needs and goals when you make a request. It can really pay off. In my case, I had to show my employers why it was in their best interest to give me a raise—because it made them money. You can often change a "no" to a "yes" if you can show what is in it for the other person.

When Ray Bradbury, the famous science-fiction writer, was twelve, he applied for a job as an announcer at a local radio station. They didn't need another announcer, certainly not a green kid with no experience. So Bradbury found out what they *did* need: someone to empty ashtrays and run errands. He offered his services in that capacity, and they took him on. Two weeks later they let him start reading the comics to children on Saturday nights. This was Bradbury's start toward his fame as a writer.

This illustrates that in giving others something they want, you'll have a better chance of receiving what *you* need. When you are trying to influence others, the promise of tangible benefits to them occasionally tips the scales in your favor. So whenever possible, offer an exchange of services or favors to the person you are approaching. It can make a big difference.

Andrew Carnegie applied this principle when in grammar school. He needed food for his baby rabbits, so he asked a few friends to go out and gather dandelions and clover. They did so eagerly. Why? The future steel magnate made them an offer they couldn't refuse: He said he would name one of the rabbits after each of them. Employing similar persuasiveness throughout his life, Carnegie went on to become one of the richest people in history.

Here are two approaches to the same request. Which is more effective?

- "Could you give us 90 days' credit on 500 components?"
  ("It's not our policy . . .")

- "If our test marketing works out, we'll need several thousand components a month. Could you give us 90 days' credit on 500?"
  ("Hmmm.")

In the second example, the person making the request has clearly spelled out the potential benefits a 90-day credit plan might bring his creditors.

The moral: Scratch the other person's back, and they'll want to scratch yours.

ALWAYS GIVE RESPECT, APPRECIATION, AND A FEELING OF WORTHINESS

In many cases you will be unable to offer the other person any tangible reward. Or the person may not expect or want anything material. You must still "give to the giver." Your currency is the spirit you convey. In other words, you should strive to make people feel good about themselves. A show of respect and appreciation can often make the toughest negotiator more pliable and more willing to satisfy your request.

In *A Life in Letters*, John Steinbeck tells about his method of bargaining for goods in Mexico. "The ordinary method," he wrote, "is to run the product down, to be horrified at the coarseness of the weave or the muddiness of the colors. But I reversed it. One serape priced at fifteen pesos I said was too beautiful. That it was impossible to give it a value in money because it was beyond any offer at all—by that time the *dueño* was nearly in tears. However, I was a poor man and if ten pesos might be accepted, not as payment but as a token of esteem, I would take the thing and love it all my life. The method aroused so much enthusiasm, not only with the *dueño* but with the market crowd, that I got it for ten without even a squeak."

When you want to get people to do something, make them feel important as well as appreciated. The following anecdote, which appeared in *Guideposts* magazine, shows what a difference such an approach can make. A young copywriter named Whit Gibson placed this ad in a local paper:

WANTED: Cleaning woman 1 day per week. Own transportation, excellent pay. Call 887-9985 after 6 P.M.

Gibson got not one response. So he called upon his professional copywriting experience and knowledge of human nature, and came up with a second ad:

WANTED: Housekeeper to take complete charge of house in country 1 day a week. Be your own boss.

Make your own decisions. Drive your own car.
Call 887-9985 after 6 P.M.

When he got home a few minutes before 6:00, the
phone was already ringing. By 7:00, nine women had
applied. Why? Notice that the second ad does not
even mention money, while the first promises "excellent pay." People like to feel important; it's worth
more than dollars to them.

In my philanthropic work, I try to answer requests
primarily on the basis of need and worthiness; but I
respond to my emotions too. I like to feel that I've
been able to help people, that I've been able to make a
difference. Here is a letter I received that allowed me
to satisfy that desire:

Dear Mr. Ross,

I'm imprisoned in Arkansas . . . I've been writing
a book about the effectiveness of punishment and
social reaction to crime. . . .

I . . . am doing everything within my power to
better myself while incarcerated. I've alienated
my family and have no friends. That's my past,
not my future.

What I would like most is a good dictionary to
help me in my writing endeavors. The problem is
it has to come from a publisher or book company. Believe it or not, this would be the most
wonderful asset in the world right now to me,
next to freedom.

J. G. W.
Tucker, Arkansas

Did I get him the dictionary? You bet! And I told him:

You've been faced with a bad situation and turned it into a positive experience. More power to you! . . . When your book gets published, I'd like to buy a copy. Good Luck!

In his letter, this man showed me how much my small gift would mean to him.

AVOID INAPPROPRIATE GIVING

When you give to the giver, be sure to give something the person wants.

Size up the individual you are approaching. What kind of tangible—or intangible—reward would mean something? If it's money, offer it if you can. If it's help with something, offer your help. If it's the use of a motorboat you own, offer the motorboat. If it's simply appreciation, then offer that. Remember, when you give to the giver, be honest; give something real. And be sensible; give something the person really does want. Don't be like the man who asked a neighbor to help him remove an oak tree, then, to show his appreciation, said, "Any time you want to use my tent and camping gear, it's yours." The problem? The neighbor did not enjoy camping.

A Wisconsin woman asked me to send her to a cooking school in Paris. "If I graduate," she said, "I'll make you the best darn meal in America. What do you say?"

What would *you* say to that offer? I answered:

I figure all that would cost about $10,000. Just think how many meals I could have at the best restaurants in America!

What this woman offered me was simply not anything I needed. On the other hand, one young man wrote me asking for a bicycle. He said, "I know you won't accept repayment for the new bike, but I will make it up to you by helping other people, as you are doing, whenever I can." Now *there* was a person who knew what I wanted, and gave it to me. And I gave him his bike.

SHOW HOW A "YES" WILL HELP YOU

Rule #4—Give in Order to Receive—also means that your request should not be selfish or greedy. What do you think of this request?

Dear Mr. Ross,

My fingernails look gross because I keep biting them when I get nervous. I'd love new acrylic nails, designed with pretty, real gold art work. They cost about $600. Will you help a cute 17-year-old?

C. B.
Hollywood, California

Can you beat that? I didn't see how granting this request would help her or anyone else. She didn't *need* acrylic nails!

On the other hand, I recently bought a cow for a couple in Washington State who needed fresh milk for their children. They had two kids of their own, and then adopted two more who had been abused by their natural parents. And I said yes to a city inspector who asked me to buy sod for an elderly couple in Florida. His request impressed me because it showed a real concern for others. The couple's backyard had been eroded by heavy rain, then dried to sand by the sun.

I don't give to self-centered causes or self-centered individuals. Few people do. You'll increase your chances of getting support from me or from anybody else by showing how the fulfillment of your request will help others as well as yourself.

People will want to help you if your purpose seems sound and good. Self-indulgent purposes rarely are. This does not mean that you cannot think of yourself and your own personal desires; you can and should. You just have to indicate that the assistance you receive will end up not only helping you, but also others. I like to help others who want to get an education, find a job, start a business of their own—people who are trying to get ahead or improve their lot, and who need a helping hand. So do most people.

SHOW THAT YOU INTEND TO GIVE YOUR ALL

If you ask for help without putting forth your best efforts, people won't be eager to assist you. Some people ask for help to escape effort: A Colorado man asked me to pay for his relocation to Australia so he could "pursue the true meaning of life." He complained that his wife would not agree to sell their house to help him "attain mental purity."

Here's a letter that reveals that same lack of effort:

Dear Mr. Ross,

At 18, I married a wonderful girl. My mother has extra room so we have been living with her for most of our marriage.

Last year we traveled to Florida by van to start a new life, but it was too hot. So, now we are back at my mother's in Wisconsin.

I am a jack-of-all-trades: construction, plumbing, and auto mechanics. Right now, I am between jobs. I like to work, but not a full eight-hour day. I would rather make a lot of money in a short time and keep my schedule open. I need a little money, so I could have some time alone and go skiing and eat at McDonald's which would help clear my thoughts.

J. S.
La Crosse, Wisconsin

Would you send this man money? I sent him something a lot more valuable (I hope)—the following advice:

Dear J.,

If you do not accustom yourself to working an eight-hour day, your schedule may be wide open. Your mother may even decide it is time for the nest to empty. Just in case you have forgotten the benefits of hard work, enclosed is a silver dollar so you won't forget what hard money looks like!

Did you ever notice, in a football game, that the passes go to the player who's ready to grab the ball and run with it? If you want others to give you what you ask for, you must show that if you get it, you will make good tracks with it.

People give a hand to those who give their all. Here is a letter from the kind of person who illustrates what I mean:

Dear Mr. Ross,

After an unsuccessful marriage and a son (he's 17 months old now), I am a single parent and must provide my own transportation and a place to live. Both my parents are deceased and I have no one to turn to. Mr. Ross, I am now 23, intelligent and willing to do any kind of work. I'm determined to fight hard in order to get a better future for my baby and me. It's not that I'm looking for a handout—just any type of work to get me started in the right direction. I'll even work on a straight commission basis in sales to prove that I can earn money for myself and my employer. I can sell anything I believe in if given the chance. Can you help me?

Mrs. A. S.
Dallas, Texas

Of course you'd help her. I did. I wrote:

Dear Mrs. S.,

I admire your attitude and willingness to work. I phoned Mrs. Myrna Walker, the personnel manager at Poly-America, Inc., in Grand Prairie. She will interview you for a position as a receptionist. If you're as determined as I think you are, this job could lead to an excellent well-paying job in sales by telephone. Mrs. Walker is expecting your phone call. Now it's up to you. Good luck.

THE PERCY ROSS IMPROVEMENT PLAN FOR PRIMING THE PUMP

Remember Jesus' saying: "Ask, and it shall be given you"? I say: "Give, and you shall receive." These two statements may seem contradictory, but they fit together like hand and glove. The way to ask effectively is to put giving into your asking.

How can you do this in your daily life? Look for opportunities to give something when you make a request, and seize them.

1. Find ways to give to the giver. Think about all the people you live with, work with, and deal with. When you ask any of them for help, favors, service, money, or other things, do you consider their desires or needs? Do you offer them tangible rewards—respect, assistance, the return of a favor, or extra effort?

Think of a request you can make in the next few days. Is there something you can give to the giver?

Take into account what you are asking for, and what is important to the person you are approaching. Then make your request.

2. *Make sure you give the right things to the giver.* During the next few days, combine an appropriate reward with your request.

3. *Find more ways to "give your all."* Think of every major area of your life. Are you giving maximum effort? Could you be giving more? The way to gain more help or support is to put in more effort. Help tends to rally around people who are active and goal-oriented.

Give more. It's a powerful way to get more. Give more to the people whose help you seek. Make the potential benefits to them very clear. Give more of yourself in all you undertake. If you do, I think you'll be surprised at the bounty you'll reap.

Chapter 7

Break Through the Barriers

All of us, at one time or another, are up against a wall when it comes to making requests. Perhaps you are standing before one right now.

The wall I'm referring to is an obstacle that keeps you from asking. When you find your nose pressed against this unyielding obstacle, you feel like keeping your mouth shut. You may be afraid to ask, or perhaps you think asking won't do any good.

Remember, in Chapter 2, the teenager from Liberia who asked to see the president of her country because she needed transportation money so that she could study in America? If you were in her position, imagine the obstacle that might have stopped you:

- "I could never get in to see the president."
- "I'm just a kid; his staff will laugh at me."
- "Even if I got in to see him, he'd probably say no."
- "I'd just be wasting my time."

Whenever you find yourself face to face with that kind of obstacle, you must either find a door through the wall, go around the wall, or break through it. Otherwise you may never get what you want in life. Which brings me to the next rule for asking:

- Rule #5   Overcome the Blocks to Asking.

There are three main walls or blocks that keep people from asking for what they need. If you do not recognize these obstacles when they appear, they can keep you from the success and happiness you seek.

THE WALL OF FEAR

There is a word in the English language that often strikes more fear in people than death itself: It is the word "no." People dread the word so much they *put off* asking for things—or never ask at all. At best, they ask with great hesitation. The following letter provides a good example of this difficulty:

Dear Mr. Ross,

I'm really scared to write this letter because I'm afraid you might not want to help our family and we have no one else to go to. See, I have eight brothers and sisters. (I'm 13 and the oldest.) Mom and Dad are divorced and he only pays child support when he feels like it. . . . Because she's been pretty sick, Mom hasn't been able to take in sewing like she used to for extra money. But the biggest problem of all is our washing

machine busted and there's no way we can get it
fixed. . . .

A. G.
Santa Rosa, California

I sent this young lady and her family a new Maytag
washing machine with a brief note: "How proud your
mother must be to have such a brave daughter as
you. . . ."

I meant it. It isn't easy to ask for something you
want or need. Too often people shrink from the or-
deal, unable to overcome the dread of being turned
down. Many people who write me confess that the
fear of rejection has kept them from writing me for
months. There are probably thousands of people I
will never hear from, because they are too apprehen-
sive to approach me. Asking takes courage.

Do you ever find yourself saying things like this to
yourself?

- "Twice she turned me down. If I ask her out
  again, she'll just say no again."
- "An order from the Smith Company would put
  me over quota. But if I ask them the wrong way, I
  may never get an order from them. Maybe I'll call
  them tomorrow, or next week."
- "I don't think I'll ask his advice. He'll probably
  tell me it's a bad idea."
- "I hate to ask for directions. They'll think I'm
  stupid. I'll just keep driving."
- "If I ask for more help, the boss may think I'm a
  slow learner."

When you really want or need something and fail to go after it, it may be because fear is getting in your way. You have to get around it or push through it to be successful. Though you turn red as a beet, feel your heart racing, or tremble in your shoes, face the problem squarely and go on. Say, "I'd like a piece of your business, Mr. Smith," or "I'd like to dance with you, Sally." Remember, if they say no, you're only as bad off as you would be if you hadn't asked at all. And if they say *yes*, you've got what you wanted!

THE WALL OF PRIDE

There's a type of pride that's good: a belief in yourself, confidence in your abilities. There's also a type of pride that's bad: a feeling that you're better than others.

This second kind of pride gets in the way of asking for help. People who suffer from it feel they should be self-sufficient. To ask is to admit they need other people, to recognize that others have power over them because they have the power to help them.

Such people carry their pride to foolish extremes. Rather than ask for directions, they may drive around lost for half an hour. They could fall to their knees with a heart attack before asking the "people next door" for help.

Lots of us find it hard to let go of this false pride. In the movie *It Happened One Night*, Claudette Colbert, who plays the part of a rich girl in trouble, cannot bring herself to ask a poor young man for help. The young man, played by Clark Gable, finally explodes in exasperation, "You couldn't just say, 'Hey, mister, couldn't you help me?' No! It would take you off your high horse!"

Don't fall into that trap. *Everyone* needs help at some point or another. Remember, most of the successful people in the world got that way because they were not afraid to ask—again and again—for help. No one can do it alone. Refusing to ask for or accept advice is not a sign of independence; it's a sign of foolhardiness.

Many people in the business world hesitate to ask "lower-level" employees for help. Their reluctance arises out of pride. Such people feel free to order or direct people to do certain things, but they resist *asking* them for help.

The president of a small manufacturing company found that his car wouldn't start one day after work. The battery was dead. He asked one of his employees, who was about to drive off, if he would give him a jump start. "If you will, you can come in half an hour late tomorrow morning," said the boss with a forced smile. He didn't like being in the position of having to ask, so he offered to "pay" the employee with time off.

Such "asking," in my opinion, is unfortunate. The president could have simply asked for help. A genuine request has dignity; it can elevate both parties. It is a transaction between equals.

In *Guideposts* magazine a few years ago there was a story about a well-to-do elderly couple whose car had a flat tire. They stopped at the side of the road, got out of their luxury sedan, and stood by helplessly. They were too proud to flag another car down and request help. A couple driving an economy car noticed their plight and stopped. The rich elderly man offered the Good Samaritans money for changing the tire, but they refused. The younger man just told them to pass the help on to the next people who needed it. Both couples took off.

Later that day the younger couple had to stop at the side of the road when their engine got overheated. They needed water, but the nearest gas station was miles ahead. In just a few minutes help was forthcoming—from the elderly couple in the luxury sedan! Smiling, the formerly "proud" gentleman produced a gallon jug of water and said, "You said to pass it on to the next person who needed help. You're it."

It's a mutual, help-each-other world. If you try to give help when you can, you'll feel more confident in asking for help when you yourself need it.

Whenever you feel a false pride rising up within you, turning you aside from your goal, push it out of the way. "I'm not one for asking," began a seventeen-year-old girl in a letter to me. I could see her pushing past her pride, though, as she went on to ask for money to buy silk roses to put on the grave of her father. He had been killed in a Thanksgiving Day auto accident two years earlier. Of course, I was glad to help out.

"I have never asked for help before," began another reader, a seventy-six-year-old Texas widow. She could not afford to paint the shabby rooms in her small retirement home. She and her husband had always been able to cope before, but now he was dead, and she needed help. How she must have wrestled with her pride before writing me! I bought the paint and asked the U.S. Air Force recruiting office in Longview to provide the labor. Sergeant Doyle Dorsey and many of his recruits came through.

False pride is a powerful barrier. It may be keeping you from asking for many things, such as:

- a promotion at work. "If the boss can't see I can handle more responsibility, I shouldn't have to tell him."
- advice from your spouse or a friend. "I should know how to handle it by myself."
- understanding or encouragement. "I'm strong; I don't need to cry on anyone's shoulder."

False pride can hold you back—both in the office and in your personal life. It isn't worth a dime; in fact, it can make you ineffective and unhappy. Watch out for it. Communicate your needs to others. You'll get a lot more of what you want in life if you do.

THE WALL OF LOW SELF-ESTEEM

The third barrier to asking is feeling unworthy of help. Many people suffer from low self-esteem. They may even consider themselves failures. Trapped by negative attitudes, they stop seeking the support of others.

If that's true of you, the first thing you've got to do is convince yourself you have something to offer. Your negative feelings are just that—feelings. Reaching out to others will actually help convince you of your inner worth. Make contact with someone who can bolster you. Let me give you an example of what I mean. Here is a letter from a reader of my column:

Dear Mr. Ross,

At 21, I married and started out in the business world with $2,500 from my family inheritance. I've worked very hard for the last 20 years, building a small, successful business—only to lose it all through some stupid mistakes. I have only myself to blame.

I'm not worried about the "friends" I lost, but more importantly I lost my confidence and self-esteem. Have you any suggestions, Mr. Ross? I'm humiliated and depressed. My family believes in me and still thinks I'm the greatest, but everyone else seems to avoid me as a "has-been."

Mr. J. J.
Shreveport, Louisiana

I answered:

Dear Mr. J.,

Better to be a "has-been" than a "never-was"! Your experience is your greatest asset. Don't give up. I've been where you are now. If you're willing to start now and show determination, you can look to me for advice.

Your situation is never hopeless. Resist negative thoughts. Think positively. If you suffer from a feeling of inferiority, practice making very small requests of people until you gain confidence. When you find many of your requests are being answered affirmatively, I think you'll gain a sense of self-worth, and be better able to ask for the more important things you need.

Perhaps you've heard of Joe Girard, the world's "number one salesman." He wasn't always a winner. Once he came to the end of his rope. He was out of work; his car was about to be repossessed, and the mortgage on his home was in danger of foreclosure. He had to use the back door of his home to avoid bill collectors. One evening his wife told him there was no food in the house for the children.

Joe Girard needed to do some asking. The next day he did. He went to a local Chevrolet dealer and pleaded for a job selling cars. The owner said he would give him a try. In the showroom, Girard phoned every friend and acquaintance he could think of, asking them to buy a car. No dice. Then, a few minutes before closing time, a man walked into the showroom. Girard grabbed him by the arm and gave him the most enthusiastic, intense sales pitch you could imagine. "I practically begged him to buy a car from me," Girard said later.

Within minutes, a miraculous thing happened. The man turned to Girard and said, "You know, I've never met anyone who *asks* the way you do—you really mean it. I'll take the car."

Girard put food on his family's table that night; and within a few years—through repeated asking—he put himself at the pinnacle of his profession. He was named the world's "number one salesman" twelve years in a row, and became the only salesperson to be listed in the *Guinness Book of World Records*.

If you feel like a failure, welcome to the club. I and just about every successful person I know has felt that way at one time or another. You may think your life is going nowhere. Don't despair. If you want your place in the sun, you've got to expect a few blisters. Take it from me—I've been burned many times. Hang in there.

Low self-esteem does not always stem from failure or difficult times. Sometimes it comes from being handicapped, or disadvantaged, from being "too young" or "too old," from being a woman, from being too tall or the "wrong" color or religion. If you are "different" in any way, you may feel inferior. This feeling may keep you from reaching out. *Don't let it*.

I have felt behind the eight ball for many reasons: because I was poor, because I was Jewish, because I never went to college. I've had to struggle with insecurities; many a time a little voice inside has said to me, "Percy, you're not good enough." I've had to fight against resentment too, but somehow I've always been able to convince myself that I'm as good as the next person. And I've found out that I *am*. So are you. If other people tell you you're not, don't believe them. Tony Dorsett, star running back for the Dallas Cowboys, once commented, "All my life I had people telling me such things as 'You're too small to be a football player' and 'You ain't gonna be nothin' but a winehead' and a lot of negative stuff like that." Rather than believing them, Dorsett developed a fighting desire to prove such people wrong. He became a superstar in the NFL, and a millionaire to boot. Looking back on his childhood, he says, "About the worst thing you can instill in a young person's mind is the notion that he's not capable of achieving something worthwhile in life."

If you suffer from low self-esteem, don't let it stop you from achieving all that you can in life. Fight back.

Pinpoint the areas where you feel inadequate. Then ask yourself: "Are my feelings standing in the way of what I want?" Look over the following list. Do you ever find yourself saying these or similar things to yourself?

- "I'm not good at that."
- "I'm out of place with people like them."
- "What's the use of trying? I'll only fail."
- "I'm too old (young, tall, dumb, ugly) . . ."
- "It's hopeless. If I ask them, they'll only say no."
- "I try to help people, but I don't like to bother them with my own problems."

If any of these remarks sound familiar, you are putting yourself down. Fight back. Remember, you're as good as anyone. You deserve success. Ask for it!

THE PERCY ROSS IMPROVEMENT PLAN FOR BREAKING THROUGH THE BARRIERS

If you hold back from asking for what you need, ask yourself why. Fear, false pride, or low self-esteem may be inhibiting you. To get past these barriers, try these two steps:

1. List situations in which you are reluctant to ask for what you need.

- Are you putting off asking for a loan to start a spare-time business? Why? Are you afraid of being turned down? Or are you afraid that getting a "yes" would force you to put your dream to the test?
- Do you need a new job but find yourself afraid to

start looking? Your friends could offer you leads and suggestions. Are you afraid to ask them? Do you feel uncomfortable or ashamed for being in this position? Do you say to yourself, "I can handle this on my own"?

On a piece of paper, write down a few situations in which you are not currently asking for what you need. Then, for each situation, decide whether it is fear, false pride, low self-esteem, or another block that is stopping you.

2. Make an attempt to overcome whatever is blocking you within the next few days. There are two good ways to get past any block: grit your teeth and ask anyway; or try to resolve the feelings that are keeping you from asking.

The first approach is the hardest. If you're willing to take the consequences, I think you'll be surprised at the number of positive responses you'll get. It takes a great deal of courage, but the results are usually worth it.

The second approach can take much longer, but it is also effective. Find another person to talk to. Then ask them to help you work up the courage or humility to go after what you need—whether it's the moon, or only a helping hand.

Follow these two steps during the next few days; and continue to try to overcome any blocks. A few are sure to get in your way. You'll feel them inhibiting you in the weeks and months ahead. Get around them. Ask when you should ask. Your future will be richer, livelier, and more rewarding if you do.

Chapter 8

Use Your Imagination

Sometimes, when you aren't getting what you want from others, it pays to call upon your imagination. If you can find a clever, offbeat, or inspired way to ask, you might be able to change a "no" into a "yes." Getting what you want in life sometimes requires the courage to try a new tack when the tried-and-true approach to your request doesn't seem to be getting you what you need. To increase your chances of getting a "yes," always remember to apply the following rule:

- Rule #6   Ask Artfully.

In the management magazine *Bits & Pieces*, published by The Economics Press, I read a story about Irvin S. Cobb. As a young man, Cobb left the farm country for New York City in high hopes of finding a job as a reporter. All the newspapers (there were several at the time) told him no positions were available.

His situation was desperate; he had a wife and a sick child to care for. Should he return home in defeat?

No. He decided to try asking for a job in a different way—a way that would capture attention and show he could write. He sent a cleverly composed letter to every editor in town. The letter ended with these words:

> This is positively your last chance. I have grown weary of studying the wallpaper design in your anteroom. A modest appreciation of my own worth forbids me doing business with your head office boy any longer. Unless you grab me right away, I will go elsewhere and leave your paper flat on its back here in the middle of a hard summer, and your whole life hereafter will be one vast, surging regret. The line forms on the right; applications considered in the order they're received. Write, wire, or call at the above address.

Cobb received four job offers the next day.

Such creative requests do not, of course, guarantee a "yes." But an unusually clever or bold request is practically guaranteed to capture attention.

A clever pitch or imaginative request can open closed doors (and minds). It can nudge someone who is on the fence into giving you a "yes." If you have been getting too many "no's" lately, try putting a little style, wit, and imagination into your request.

CLEVERNESS CAN CONVINCE

A clever request not only arouses curiosity; it can also frequently overcome resistance or opposition. For example, one summer a Red Cross worker in Minneapolis was looking for a way to get more people to donate blood. In a flash of inspiration, she made up the following sign and posted it on the front of the building:

BEFORE GOING ON VACATION, DONATE BLOOD.
MOSQUITOES DON'T GIVE COFFEE AND
DOUGHNUTS—WE DO.

As a result, many more people that month stopped in to give blood.

Max Schling, a New York City florist, stimulated sales by running an unusual ad in the *New York Times*. It was entirely in shorthand. Curious businessmen asked their secretaries for a translation. The copy read: "Remember Schling when the boss needs flowers for the wife."

A clever or imaginative request is often memorable, and can make more of an impression on others. A supervisor in a plant where television sets were being assembled asked employees to avoid mistakes and watch quality only to find his request falling on deaf ears. After giving the problem some thought, he posted a sign that read as follows:

CAREFUL!
This may be
the set
YOU
get!

As a result, there was an immediate drop in mistakes on the line.

An imaginative argument or request can turn the

tide. Let me give you another example. If you had received the two letters below, would you have been more likely to say "yes" to the first or the second?

Dear Mr. Ross,

I'm a 13-year-old girl. I made cheerleader this year, but Mom and Dad are out of work and can't afford to buy me shoes. They cost $46.95. Will you help?

Dear Mr. Ross,

I'm a 13-year-old girl. Lucky me . . . I made cheerleader this year. Unlucky me . . . Mom and Dad are out of work, and they can't afford to buy me shoes. They cost $46.95. Will you help?

You'd probably want to say "yes" to *both* requests; I would. The second letter, though, has a bit more spirit and would be more apt to catch the reader's eye, don't you agree?

Such cleverness can be inappropriate at times, however. You don't want to attempt to be clever in the wrong situation. But keep in mind that a light touch or an imaginative approach can pave the way at times to a positive response.

TRY HUMOR

Sometimes humor can help frame your request. It can help to disarm the person you are approaching, especially in cases where a bald request might bring an angry or poorly considered response. Humor is often one of the most powerful and effective weapons at your disposal.

George Washington used humor effectively to convince the Constitutional Convention that a resolution to restrict the standing army to 5,000 men didn't make sense. He told the Convention that he could agree to the 5,000-man limit—if the Convention would also limit the size of any invading army to 3,000 troops. There was laughter and no need of debate. A direct attack on the resolution would likely have provoked a time-consuming argument.

If you can make people smile or laugh, you've already halfway convinced them of your point of view. Humor, if even just a faint smile, cheers people up and makes them more open and accepting. In one seaside town, for example, many stores displayed signs that read: NO BARE FEET. The proprietor of one store put up a sign with the opposite message: BARE FEET WELCOME. The store sold sandals. People smiled, and many people bought.

TRY AN END RUN

When direct requests don't work, it often pays to take a different tack. Think about the problem at hand, and try to come up with another way to go at it. George Horace Lorimer, longtime editor of the *Saturday Evening Post*, used to reject many of the sketches submitted by Norman Rockwell, the famous illustrator of *Post* covers. Rockwell noticed that

Lorimer always accepted three sketches, rejecting all others, no matter how good the other five or ten were.

Rockwell might have argued with Lorimer, but he decided to try an end run. He started bringing in only five sketches each time—three of which he really liked. He enthused over these to Lorimer, and referred to the other two critically. Lorimer would say "Good" to each of the three Rockwell had praised, and reject the other two. Rockwell carried off this scheme for many years, selling Lorimer on precisely the covers he wanted.

Juliette Low, founder of the Girl Scouts, used an end-run approach when asking women to become Scout leaders. She played on the fact that she was hard-of-hearing. Whenever someone would say she was too busy or unqualified, Low would pretend she didn't hear, and would continue to "sell" the virtues of scouting with great enthusiasm. The objections usually evaporated.

Roundabout methods of asking can be effective in the right situation. Sometimes it's simply easier to go around an obstacle than through it.

One of the greatest masters of roundabout persuasion was Ben Franklin. When he wanted to gain cooperation from a political enemy, he avoided direct discussion. Instead he would ask the man to lend him a certain rare book from his library. Flattered, the man would begin to act more kindly toward Franklin, making Franklin's job easier when he actually made his pitch.

One of the most effective ways to approach people who are likely to be cantankerous is to appeal to their ego or self-importance. A company owned by Andrew

Carnegie manufactured an alternative to the Pullman sleeping car. The steel magnate proposed to George Pullman that their two companies merge, explaining the merits of such a maneuver. Pullman expressed doubt. Then Carnegie suggested that the new firm be named "The Pullman Palace Car Company." Pullman smiled, and they shook hands on the deal.

Sometimes coming at a problem from the side can bring you a "yes" when a frontal attack will bring only resistance.

Less effective:	(to your spouse): "How about going away for the weekend?"
More effective:	"I'd love to be alone with you this weekend."
Less effective:	(to your boss): "It takes too much time to fill out the call reports. We ought to simplify the form."
More effective:	"The other day you said we need to spend more time with customers. Well, I think I know how to find an extra hour a week. If we simplified . . ."

TRY ASKING WITH MORE THAN JUST WORDS

In going after what you want in life, don't limit yourself to talking or writing. Ask with your actions, too. Charles Brower wanted a job with the George Batten advertising agency. After two years of trying, he was rewarded with an offer—but the man who made the offer was himself fired just before Brower's starting day. Nobody at the firm had a record that he had been hired, and it looked as if he was out of the job he'd wanted so much. He might have argued, but instead he simply found a spare office, acted like a new employee, and started giving people a hand. Within three weeks, management got used to him, and began giving him paychecks! Several years later Brower rose to the top of the agency, now known as Batten, Barton, Durstine & Osborn.

Eddie Rickenbacker "asked" for a job in a similar fashion. One morning he simply walked into an automotive manufacturing company and began cleaning up the metal shavings, dirt, and grease. Taken aback but impressed, the owners let him stay. Rickenbacker's persuasiveness and enthusiasm eventually led him to establish Eastern Airlines.

There are many ways that you can ask for things without using words. For example, instead of asking for a new responsibility at work, simply begin "helping" in that area. Sometimes actions speak louder, and more eloquently, than words.

TRY DIFFERENT ANGLES

Use your creativity and be flexible in making requests. If one approach doesn't work, try another. Screenwriter Daniel O'Bannon had trouble placing the original script for the science fiction movie *Alien*. Every major studio, including Twentieth Century–Fox, rejected it. Still believing in his script,

O'Bannon decided to approach Fox a second time, but from a different angle. He smuggled a copy of the script into an office frequented by the studio's main writer-directors. One of these people, Walter Hill, found the script with an attached note, "Please read this." Hill did, liked it, and got his colleagues to accept it after a few changes.

There are many routes to the "yes" you seek. Look for offbeat avenues to acceptance. I know of an insurance salesman in Nova Scotia who came up with an unusual solution to a bad day he was having. No one seemed to want his product. He noticed some workmen on a scaffold outside an office building. He wrote a note and held it up to the window: "Would you be interested in some life, accident, or disability insurance?" The men said they would listen to his pitch if he would come out on the scaffold with them. He did, and one of them bought a $50,000 policy.

You can transform many a bad situation into a good one if you think creatively. In the early 1700s, the great French philosopher Voltaire was walking down a London street. Many Englishmen of that day hated the French with a passion. Some bystanders recognized him and began shouting, "Kill him! Hang the Frenchman!"

Instead of running or begging for his life, Voltaire said, "Englishmen! You want to kill me because I am a Frenchman. Am I not punished enough, in not being an Englishman?" Pacified and flattered, they began cheering, and escorted him safely to his destination.

Here's another example of creative thinking from my own life. In 1951 a New York fur dealer gave me a bad check for $25,000. That blow, plus a slowdown in the fur industry, knocked my business for a loop. As a result my company went under, and I was flat broke.

I needed money fast and thought I could get it by using my skill as an auctioneer. I searched desperately through the newspaper for something I could auction—automobiles, trucks, tractors, anything. Finally I saw an ad placed by a contractor who had $100,000 worth of used construction equipment for sale. I went to see him—his name was Byron Clark—and asked if I could serve as an auctioneer on his behalf. Mr. Clark said, "Fine," but he couldn't pay the 15- to 20-percent commission I needed to make a profit. The most he could afford was 5 percent which was too little for me.

I left his yard very disappointed, because I really needed the money. I was halfway home when an inspiration hit me. I could approach the situation from a different angle.

I turned around and drove back to Mr. Clark. I asked if he had friends and associates who also had equipment they wanted to sell. "Sure," he said, "I know several other contractors who do. I was off to the races.

Instead of holding a $100,000 auction for one seller, I accumulated $1 million worth of used heavy equipment from thirty-seven different sellers. I charged only 5 percent commission, but I made $50,000—a small fortune to me at the time. Not only did I have cash for my immediate needs, but I had found myself a new business. For the next eight years, I organized used heavy-equipment auctions from coast to coast. I was on my way to becoming a millionaire.

When you don't get a "yes," when people don't respond as you'd like, put your brain into gear. Think of a new approach, a new proposition, a new offer, or a new way to ask. It can make all the difference in the world.

THE PERCY ROSS IMPROVEMENT PLAN FOR USING YOUR IMAGINATION

If you're not getting the support you expect and want, put some imagination into your requests. You may open some doors that would otherwise remain closed—and one of those doors just might lead to a whole new life.

1. List a few situations in which people aren't giving you what you want or need. These situations could relate to money, advancement at work, educational opportunities, relationships with the opposite sex, family matters:

- "The boss won't accept my suggestions."
- "Jamie won't clean her room."
- "I haven't been able to interest any investors in my new business."

2. Think of new ways to ask for what you want. Pick one or more of the troublesome situations on your list. Then figure out how to approach things differently. Consider using cleverness, humor, an indirect approach, or nonverbal means.

For example, figure out how to make your boss laugh at the existing procedure before suggesting an improvement; or get Jamie's attention by transforming her "problem" into an "opportunity."

3. Ask, and see what happens. Put your new approach into action. You may still get a "no," but even if you do, you will have improved your ability to make requests. Best of all, you may find that your new approach is exactly what you needed to get what you wanted.

Chapter 9

What Not to Do

No matter what you're after—a promotion, a bank loan, or simply time with a special person—if you ask for it, you stand a chance of getting it. But if you don't ask for it in the right way, the odds of getting it will be stacked against you.

There are two big mistakes people make in going after what they want. They are the biggest mistakes you can make. The first is to *demand* whatever it is you want. The second is to *beg* for it. To ask correctly, always keep in mind and apply the next rule of asking:

- Rule #7   Request or Invite; Never Demand or Beg.

There is a proverb that I discovered early on in life, which orginated in Madagascar (Malagasy Republic): "The dog's bark is not might, but fright." When you "bark" or demand something, usually it's because you're afraid—afraid of being turned down. Unfortunately, making demands of people is one of the least efficient, and least successful, ways of getting what you want.

Let me give you an example of what I mean. Early in her career, Jean Stapleton, who later played the wife of Archie Bunker in the TV series *All in the Family*, won a bit part in a play. That didn't make her very happy. She thought she deserved the starring role. Sometime later, the leading lady broke her leg and Jean asked if she could take over the part. The director told her she could fill in, but only until he found somebody else. "Somebody else!" protested Jean, her resentment boiling over. "But what about me? I can play the part!"

How would you have responded to Jean's outburst if you were the director? Would you have said, "Well, since you feel so strongly about it, you can have the part?" I doubt it. In fact, the director said, "No. You're too young." Jean thought he was being unfair and stalked off angrily.

If you were an actor or actress in a situation like Jean's, what would you have done? What is the right way to approach the director in this situation? I believe you should simply ask for the part good-naturedly, and *make a good case for yourself*. Then you've done all you can. If the director turns you down, accept it without ill will. Do the very best you can in the bit part, and let it be known you're eager for something bigger. People will respect you for your eagerness and ambition. If the answer is "no" for the moment, it may become a "yes" down the line.

This is exactly what Jean Stapleton did. The day she was turned down, she went home all riled up. That night she thought and prayed, and finally let go of her angry feelings. She didn't *have* to have the lead, she decided. She would work hard in the part as long as she had it. Her new attitude made a world of difference; the director appreciated her willingness to cooperate. She filled in for the departing star, and did an excellent job. The director still felt he wanted someone older. He found another star, and Jean kept on working like a trouper in her supporting role— until one day the director told Jean that the new actress wasn't working out. Jean could have the lead. "I still think you're too young for it, but you did a good job," he said. "The part's yours."

Jean Stapleton's career went straight up from there. But how far do you think she would have gotten if she had stayed angry, harassed the director about the lead, and treated her bit part as an insult? Jean realized she had made a *request*—and that carried the possibility of being turned down. When she *was* turned down, she decided to live with it, and make the best of it.

Making a *demand* is very different from making a request. When you ask for something, you show respect for the other person's right to say no. The other person has options, choices. You are not giving the person an ultimatum. If the other person decides to honor your request, he or she can feel good about it. The person has *given* you something. He or she has made a decision, not a concession. Both sides feel they have won. When you are making a demand, however, you make it very hard for the other person to say no—or yes. In effect, you are making a veiled threat. Either the other person gives you what you want, *or else*:

- You'll be unhappy, maybe quit, cut off the relationship, etc.;
- You'll make them "pay" by giving them the cold shoulder, or denying something to them in the future;
- You'll make them feel guilty.

In other words, you are putting the other person on the spot. You are not truly *asking*. The element of choice, the option to say "no" is being taken away. This is *not* an effective way to get what you want. Let me give you an example of what I mean.

As I mentioned in Chapter 2, a woman wrote to me "requesting" $25,000. One morning, when Connie Hanson, my longtime assistant, came into the office, the phone was ringing. When she answered it, she heard a woman angrily ask, "Where the hell have you been? I've been trying to reach you for two hours."

Miss Hanson replied, "Wait one moment, please. May I just say good morning, and ask who is calling?"

The irate woman replied, "I'm Mrs. Baker [not her real name] from New York!"

Then Miss Hanson said, "You must remember there is a one-hour time difference here. It's later in New York than in Minneapolis. Our office opens in fifteen minutes. But since I'm here, I will be happy to answer any questions you have. Would you tell me the nature of your call?"

"I wrote Mr. Ross a letter last week and told him I needed $25,000 by this Friday. And I haven't heard a damn word from him!"

Miss Hanson was taken aback, but kept her cool. "What do you need the money for?" she asked.

The reply had the charm of a rattlesnake's hiss. "It's none of your goddamn business! Who the hell are you to question why I need $25,000?"

"I'm Mr. Ross's assistant, and I don't like being spoken to that way."

"Tough!" snapped the woman.

I think by now you can guess how much money I sent her. People who try to get what they want by demanding it are simply not using their heads. And they're not likely to get what they want.

THE DIFFERENCE BETWEEN DEMANDING AND ASKING

Every time you demand something you are attempting to rob someone—rob them of their freedom of choice. Nobody likes to give in to demands. And even if they have to, they do so grudgingly, with resentment. One manager I know who runs a small manufacturing company, for example, yells and screams at his employees whenever they make a mistake. He *demands* that they do the job correctly, without mistakes, and threatens to fire them if they don't. Unfortunately, while he solves the problem for the moment, somehow mistakes keep cropping up. The workers feel abused, and morale is very low. The company's productivity has actually gone down.

Another businessman I know follows a completely different approach. When an employee makes a mistake, the manager often gets angry, but not with the employee—with himself. "Damn!" he says. "I should have checked that before you finished the job." He figures it's his fault for not supervising properly. By casting blame on himself, the manager avoids laying blame on his employees and avoids making unreasonable demands of them. His employees, seeing what they themselves did wrong, try all that much harder to do better the next time. Morale stays high, and there are few mistakes. Each employee takes responsibility for his or her own job, and makes a conscious decision to improve things.

Here are a few "requests" that are actually veiled demands:

- "Bob, you've *got* to lend me $100."
  ("Then why ask—why not just take it?")
- "Mrs. Tyler, I've been working here five years. If I don't get that new supervisor's job, I'm going to be very upset."
  ("I was going to give it to you, Phil, but since that's the way you feel about it . . .")
- "Say, Marsha, you're my kind of girl. I'm taking you to the dance Saturday. I'll pick you up about eight."
  ("How can I get out of this?")

Demands like these are not likely to help you achieve your goal. To get what you want out of life, you've got to learn how to ask for things in the right way.

People who know how to ask properly take care to respect the other person's free will. For example, of the people who write me as a result of my column, those who know how to ask often include a statement like this: "Thanks for reading this letter, whether you can help me or not." They show respect for my right to decide. They state their case or situation matter-of-factly, without trying to manipulate me.

Here are the three demands given above, presented as sincere requests, in the most favorable light:

- "Bob, could you possibly lend me $100?"
  ("Maybe. What's up?")
- "Mrs. Tyler, I've enjoyed working with you these past five years. I hope you'll consider me for that new supervisor's position. I'd really like the responsibility."
  ("Glad to hear it, Phil. As a matter of fact, I've been thinking of you for it.")
- "Say, Marsha, would you like to go out with me sometime? There's a great movie playing this weekend."
  ("Sounds like fun.")

The person being asked has the opportunity to say no. And it's important to remember that the answer to your request *may be* just that! If so, you can try asking someone else (if someone else can give you what you want) or you can accept the "no" for the time being, and try again later when circumstances have changed. If you've asked for a raise, and your boss turns you down, work hard and try him or her again several months down the line, when you can show you're worth more. If you're asking someone out for a date, and he or she turns out not to be free, try them again for some special event you know they'd like to attend.

HOW TO TELL A DEMAND FROM A REQUEST

There may be times when you're not sure whether you're making a demand or a request. It's not always easy to tell the difference between the two. Ask yourself these questions:

- Can I cheerfully accept being turned down?
- Am I using any kind of pressure to force a "yes" answer?

Sometimes people start out asking for something in a perfectly straightforward way, but when they begin to realize the person is about to turn them down, launch into an "attack." Take, for example, the case of a teenager asking to use her father's car:

> "May I borrow the car tonight, Dad?"
>
> "Sorry, Rachel, not after that ticket you got for speeding."
>
> "But, Dad, I have to go to dancing class! Meg drove the last three times. It's not fair for her to have to drive again."

In this case, Rachel may actually get the car. A demand *can* work—in the short run. But though her father may give in, he's not going to like it. And he very likely will *not* give her the car another time, perhaps the one time Rachel wants it most. That's the problem with demands: Even if you do get what you want, you've created a "win-lose" situation. The person who meets your demands feels like a loser. This often creates bad feelings that can affect future dealings, when you may end up losing.

Think about all the areas of your life: work, home, school, community affairs, recreation, friendships. Do you make true requests of the people you deal with? Or do you try to push or manipulate them into things? Demands tend to take one of two forms:

1) Abusiveness. People are afraid to get a "no," so they shout and scream in a desperate attempt to get a "yes." They are trying to stack the odds in their favor. Unfortunately, they usually do just the opposite. Have you ever argued with a hotel clerk for a room, or a restaurant hostess for a table in a crowded restaurant? Screaming and shouting usually get you nowhere, except out the door. A reasonable request, however, might just get you what you want.

2) Threats. If you suggest that bad things might happen to the other person if you get turned down, you are making a threat. For example:

- "If you let me have the car tonight, Dad, I'll be really nice to you."
  (Translation: "If you don't let me have it, I'll be rotten.")
- "If you give me the raise I've asked for, I'll promise to work very hard."
  (Translation: "If you don't give me the raise, I won't work very hard.")

Do you feel compelled to add a bit of "convincing" to your requests? Do you ever put a little "bite" into them? If so, you are likely making a veiled demand. Be very careful how you phrase your request. The way to truly get what you want is not to demand— but to ask.

DON'T GO BEGGING

To go back to the Jean Stapleton anecdote for a moment, let's look at another approach Jean might have taken with the director when she was turned down for the lead. She might have pleaded with him: "Please, I've been playing bit parts for such a long time. I'm good. If you don't let me have the lead, my whole future could be ruined. You're a nice, considerate man. If you let me have the lead, I'll never, ever forget it. Won't you *please* give me a break?"

Too often, people making a request resort to this approach. They beg and plead for what they want. Do you think *this* approach would have gotten Jean the part?

Not likely. The director probably would have thought her weak and undeserving of the part. Begging, even more than familiarity, breeds contempt.

Recently I noticed a wealthy woman arriving at an airport when several flights had been delayed because of bad weather. The woman tried to talk her way into the front of a long line at the check-in counter. "Won't one of you nice people let me in?" she said. "I just can't be late to my niece's coming-out party," she begged piteously. Finally someone did let her in, and the rest of the people in the line booed her. They too had places to go, and I'm sure some of them had better reasons for arriving on time than she did. That woman couldn't have had much self-respect, and I know most of the people in line had no respect for her at all. You can be sure that her "begging" ploy wouldn't have worked a second time.

Begging seems very different from demanding, but it is really just the opposite side of the coin. In fact, begging can *be* a kind of demand. When you beg or plead to get the things you want, you are once again trying to circumvent the other person's right to say "no." Your weapon is the other person's often over-developed sense of guilt. But begging is rarely effective. It can rarely turn a decided "no" into a "yes," and it simply demeans you and betrays your sense of insecurity.

BUTTERING SOMEONE UP

Many people do not realize they are begging. They may inject a note of false flattery into their request without even realizing what they are doing. Do you ever butter people up to get them to do something? Take, for example, the case of an elderly man whose cat is stuck in a tree. He calls out to a young boy next door, "Billy, you're such a nice, considerate young man. Would you mind getting my cat out of the tree?" The extra flattery that preceded the man's request was intended to manipulate the young boy into answering "yes." And in this case given the circumstances, Billy probably did help the man out. But Billy probably felt somewhat used, coerced into saying yes. The elderly man forced himself upon Billy with a request that smacked of begging. And you can guess who will make every effort *not* to be around the next time his neighbor has another "request."

If the neighbor were truly *asking* Billy, he would have said something like this: "Billy, would you do me a favor? My cat's up the tree and I can't get it down. Would you help me?"

How do you know if you're buttering someone up? How can you tell if you are imploring or beseeching—begging—rather than making a straight request? For one thing, if you are asking for something from someone face to face, you may feel a false flattering smile spring to your face. Your shoulders may slump a bit, so that you can literally "look up" to your victim. You may find yourself nodding a lot, or agreeing with anything the other person says. You may laugh at jokes that aren't funny; and avoid saying anything that might smack of disagreement.

Because you want something from the other person, you are willing to temporarily sacrifice your equality and dignity, and put yourself in a lesser position to get it. Unfortunately, the tactic rarely works, and even when it does, you can be sure that the other person is aware of your actions. You will be less respected for it, and it can prove fatal in a relationship or in your attempt to climb up the corporate ladder. At best, you might win the battle, only to lose the war. It's just not worth it, either from the point of view of your independence, or your ultimate goals.

WHINING AND COMPLAINING

Whining and complaining to get what you want is another form of begging. We've all run into the kind of person who says peevishly, *"Why can't I get this?"* or *"Why don't you ever do that?"* The answer, of course, is that they don't know how to ask for things properly. Such a powerless posture *deserves* a negative response, and usually gets one. Here are a few examples of requests that are made in the form of complaints:

- "You kids are driving me crazy. Can't you ever give me any peace and quiet?"

- "Everyone else on the block has a stereo. Why can't I have one?"
- "It's too hot in here to concentrate. Why even bother trying to work in this heat without proper air conditioning?"

The problem with these "requests" is that no one takes them very seriously. Change those sad, self-righteous laments into positive requests, and you'll be amazed at the results! Here are those same remarks, but presented in a way that will increase your chances of getting what you want:

- "Kids, I'd like a little quiet time to myself right now. Please go outside and play for an hour or two."
- "Mom, I would really like to have a stereo to keep on top of all the new groups. Could you help me? I'll pay you back."
- "Boy, it's hot in here, and it's begun to affect our work. We need to do a good job, but it's hard to maintain productivity in this heat. Would you consider fixing or replacing the air conditioner?"

Remember, begging and demanding are two sides of the same coin—they are attempts to manipulate other people by taking away their option to say "no." My advice is simple: When you want something, just ask. Present your case, and make your request simply, with a positive frame of mind. There is always a temptation to resort to manipulation or begging but *don't* give in to it. Ask with a smile on your face. Ask eye-to-eye, equal to equal, with your head held high.

A request is an honest transaction, free of guilt. The other party is always free to accept or reject it, according to his or her needs or judgment. And you should not feel ashamed to ask for what you want or need.

Let me give you an example from my own life. One summer when I was sixteen, I was hitchhiking back home from an ROTC camp. I had only 50 cents in my pocket, and I was famished. I didn't want to spend my coins on food, because I needed them for a phone call in case of an emergency. In Marquette, Michigan, while waiting for my next ride, I was desperate for a little food. I entered a restaurant and asked the waitress at the counter, "Could you please let me have a glass of hot water?"

The waitress was a nice woman with a smile on her face. "Certainly," she said.

"Thanks," I replied. "Is there any charge?"

"No," she said, and I sat down at the counter and poured catsup into the glass. It was the best tomato soup I ever tasted.

Was that begging? I didn't lower my head; I didn't ask for pity. Nor did I demand help or try to manipulate her in any way. I asked politely for what I wanted, and I received it.

I have never felt shame for asking for what I wanted in life, and I have asked for plenty of things when I was in pretty desperate straits. I have been turned down occasionally, but I've also made three fortunes, and have received a good portion of what I've asked for.

I'd like to share a letter that I received as a result of my column, from a person truly in need who knew how to ask for assistance. Notice how forthright, proud, and honest the request is. There is no hint of begging or demanding in it.

Dear Señor Ross,

Me, my wife, and three kids come here to Palm Springs from Tijuana, Mexico, four years ago. I work as gardener and save up enough money so last year I buy a old '73 Ford pickup to go in business myself.

I made terrible mistake by not looking at truck careful to see if in good shape. Man who sold me pickup got in bad trouble with law. No way can he take care of fixing to make run good. Engine need work, radiator leaks, tires bad, and transmission no good. Fix-up is $1,400. Must work two years to save that much money. I worry much about money to fix. I get no credit from bank or garage. You help me? I pay back. Gracias.

E. R.
Palm Springs, California

This man admitted his mistake, and I didn't get the feeling he admitted it to make points. He wasn't trying to put something over on me. He was just describing his situation. He wasn't asking for pity or a handout. He wasn't demanding assistance. He was simply asking for a helping hand. This was my reply:

Dear Mr. R.,

I phoned Bob Closson, owner of the Palm Springs Texaco Station on N. Palm Canyon Drive. Call him and he will arrange for towing your pickup into his shop. He will do everything necessary to put it in good running order. Gracias to Mr. Closson, because he wants to help and will contribute to half of the bill. I will pick up the other half.

THE PERCY ROSS IMPROVEMENT PLAN FOR LEARNING WHAT NOT TO DO

If you feel you unconsciously beg or demand when you make a request, here are a few tips you might use to overcome these bad habits. By following these tips, you can set up your own improvement plan. I think you'll be amazed by your success.

1. List situations in which you now demand or beg when you are trying to get the things you want. Be specific. Write down the situations, the people involved, all the relevant details.

2. Practice changing your approach. Before you make a request, particularly one that means a lot to you, practice making it in advance. Does it seem straightforward, or are there hints of demanding or begging in it? Keep practicing until you get it right. Be careful to pick appropriate words or phrases.

3. Try out your new approach. Select situations in which you must ask for someone's help or cooperation. See if your new approach makes a difference. Start out with situations in which the outcome isn't crucial—if you find yourself falling into old habits, stop and start again. In time, making effective, positive requests without begging or demanding will come naturally.

When I made my living as an auctioneer many years ago, I always started off with a smile. That was important. Of course, an auctioneer is a person who asks people for money constantly. I would ask, "What am I bid?" Often no one would say anything, and I would have to keep asking. I would do it in a good-natured, even humorous way. I always had a positive attitude. I might coax people to make a bid, but I never begged. Often someone would start off the bidding with a ridiculously low amount, fifty cents or a dollar. I would smile and thank them. I never put anyone down, no matter how low the bid. I never insulted anyone. Soon higher and higher bids would come. And in the end, I was quite successful as an auctioneer.

Remember, as you go on in your career, and in your life, to apply Rule #7. Ask correctly—request or invite. If you do, I think you'll see more positive results.

Chapter 10

The Best People
Do It

For years comedian Rodney Dangerfield has been saying, "I don't get no respect." We laugh because we know how he feels; we often "don't get no respect" either.

Everybody hungers for appreciation, courtesy, consideration—the niceties that say, "I respect you; I think you're an important, worthwhile human being." If you want people to say "yes" to you, don't neglect the eighth rule of asking:

- **Rule #8   Show Respect.**

When Georges Clemenceau, the great French premier, was traveling by car to the Versailles Peace Conference, his young secretary said he was sick and tired of diplomatic courtesy. "It's nothing but a lot of hot air," he complained. Clemenceau answered, "All etiquette is hot air, but that's what's in our automobile tires and see how it eases the bumps."

Etiquette, courtesy, respect—call it what you will—eases all types of human bumps, jolts, and friction. It makes people think a little more kindly toward you, warms them up to your proposition, opens their minds to your needs or interests. No matter what you want from others, you're more likely to get it if you show a little respect.

SINCERE RESPECT IS BEST

I often speak to children in classrooms, churches, or synagogues. I tell them the five most important words in the English language are *please*, *thank you*, and *I'm sorry*. "If you use these five words with a firm handshake," I say, "you're on your way to becoming more successful in whatever you do."

I mean it. Showing respect has smoothed my own way to success and wealth. When I was a boy, I used courtesy and respect when selling eggs door-to-door. I would often ask people how they felt. My father taught me to give compliments. When I collected money from my father's delinquent customers, I was careful never to show the slightest sign of disrespect or disapproval. I would smile and say, "If you can't afford anything this time, it's okay. Maybe next time." This approach almost never failed me. The customers would always give me something.

Learn to say *please*, and mean it; to say *thank you*, and mean it; to say *I'm sorry*, and mean it; to show respect in dozens of other ways, and mean it.

Genuine respect means a lot to me; I think it means a lot to everyone. One of my favorite books is *How to Win Friends and Influence People* by Dale Carnegie.

Some of my acquaintances look down their noses at Carnegie because they think he tells people to use tricks—a fake smile, phony compliments, a glad hand—to get their way. But I don't think he does. His first rule of human relations is "Become genuinely interested in other people." Note that word *genuinely*. His sixth rule is "Make the other person feel important—and do it sincerely." Note that word *sincerely*. All of his rules, though susceptible to abuse, are intended to be applied from the heart. Showing respect works best when it's real, when you feel it and give it from deep inside.

SAY "PLEASE"

Please is more than just a word; it's also a concept. It means "Such and such would please me, if it would please you to do it." The idea behind saying please, in words or as a concept, is mutual pleasure.

By saying "please" you offer the promise of enjoyment—at least a bit of it—on both sides. This is the reason "please," properly said, makes people more willing to say "yes."

We've all heard a child at the dinner table say, "Pass the salt," or "Give me the butter." Sometimes they get the salt or the butter, but more often they get a reprimand: "Say 'please'" or "Get it yourself" or "Haven't you learned any manners?"

Getting across the idea of shared happiness and respect is the important thing. And you don't have to use the word *please* to accomplish this. A request such as "Would you pass me the salt, Jane?" does the job by implication.

Read the following requests. Which ones, in your judgment, get across the idea of *please*?

- "You should place your order by Friday, Mr. Jones, or we may be out of stock."
- "May I please take the exam again, Miss Bowen? You've got to let me; I don't want to flunk."
- "If you don't mind lending out your chain saw, Fred, I sure could use it Saturday morning."
- "Change the channel, would you?"

The first sentence is a warning. The second uses the word *please* but violates its spirit. The third and fourth could get across the idea of mutual pleasure if said in the right tone of voice.

Saying "please" can make a big difference. When I was caught buying stolen scrap metal, I asked the property owner, Mr. Davis, to give me a second chance; and I put a big implied "please" into my request. I said, "If you don't press charges against me, I promise I'll never do this again." My words, my manner, and my tone of voice said in so many words, "My future is in your hands. If it would please you to do this for me, it sure would please me."

Always get across the idea of *please*, no matter what you're asking for. It really pays. A salesman I know was trying to sell plastic resin to the president of a company that made ball-point pens. He made a very strong pitch—too strong, he realized. In pointing out the superior quality and reasonable cost of his product, he made the president feel defensive—as if he *had* to buy the resin or admit he was stupid. There was a long silence after the salesman asked for the order. Then, in a flash of inspiration, he smiled and added the key word, "please." The president, given a little breathing room, laughed and said "yes."

SAY "THANK YOU"

"Thank you" isn't just a nice thing to say after you've been given something. It's also a tool for influencing people. There are three times when it's smart to say "thank you": when you're asking for something before you get an answer; after you get an answer (whether it's "yes" or "no"); and after you benefit from a "yes."

It's courteous to thank people in advance. Doing so also gives potential givers a bit of appreciation, a foretaste of the gratitude they'll get if they say "yes."

Many people who write me for help thank me in advance. Here's an example:

Dear Mr. Ross,

I'm 14 and the oldest of four sisters. I hope you can help Mom and us. Dad left about a year ago and we don't know where he is. Mom doesn't have any money left from her welfare check to buy us some used clothes and shoes from Goodwill Industries.

Thirty-five dollars would sure help us. I'm old enough to do some baby-sitting soon and will pay you back little by little, I promise.

Mom, me, and my sisters thank you, Mr. Ross, for even reading our letter.

A. M.
Santa Rosa, California

I replied:

Dear A.,

There are a lot of good people in this world. Mrs.
K. of Philadelphia sent me $200 for "a deserving
family." I've endorsed it over to you and along
with it is another check from me for $200.

The advance "thank you" was not the only reason I
said yes, but it helped. It showed me this young lady
had a lot of consideration and a lot of heart. How
could I resist wanting to help her?

Another time a Washington man asked me for $200
to pay his union dues; he couldn't pay them because
he was out of work. He ended his letter, "Thank you
for your time and anything you can help with." I sent
him the $200 and suggested that once he got on his
feet, he might help another union member who was
in the same fix.

When you get an answer to your request, say
"thank you." It's surprising how many people fail to
do this. You might not believe it, but when I give
money or items of need to people, I sometimes never
hear from them again. This lack of response is disap-
pointing, so I'm doubly pleased when people take the
trouble to express their gratitude. This letter from a
young man in Texas really made my day:

Dear Friend Percy Ross,

Thank you for the bike! I knew you liked to go
first class, but I never expected a 10-speed bicycle! Now when I want to go somewhere special, I
can. I really want to be a millionaire like you. I

applied for a job as a lifeguard and they accepted me. I'm eager and excited. I started work after my indoctrination session. I never could have done it without you. . . .

I know you won't accept repayment for the new bike, but I will make it up to you by helping other people, as you are doing, whenever I can.

M. N.
Dallas, Texas

I think I'm just like most people who give a helping hand to others. I'm grateful for appreciation; a "thank you" is like the frosting on the cake.

Often I am criticized for my public style of giving; many people think it is better to give anonymously. In one of my columns I offered the following explanation:

I often wonder about those who criticize my style of sharing. Do they remain "anonymous" when giving flowers, gifts, or cash on birthdays and anniversaries? I'll bet they sign their names and delight in the pleasure they give.

I wonder if they hide in another room when their children open their presents on Christmas morning. I'll bet they really enjoy the thank you's, smiles, hugs, and kisses . . . just as I do.

Let me pass on an interesting fact from a man who administers educational grants. "Aside from a worthy cause," he said, "the thing that motivates the foundation more than anything else is acknowledgment for helping make a difference. The successful grant seekers make clear just how the foundation will be given credit."

Give thanks. Say it, write it, or phone it. Givers *want* to hear it. It really makes a difference to them; it gives them the spirit to go on giving.

Say thank you, too, when you get a "no." Why? Because it makes the other person feel better, and it may help you to get a "yes" in the future. Many times in business, after being turned down, I have said "Thanks for your time" or "Thanks for listening to me" or "I really appreciated your comments and suggestions." Very often these "exit thank you's" have kept doors open. More than once new opportunities have walked through those same doors.

There's another time when it's a good idea to say "thank you": after you've gotten a "yes" and enjoyed the fruits of it for a time. Letters like this make my day:

Dear Mr. Ross,

I want to thank you very much for supplying me with two hearing aids that I really needed. . . . I'm glad I waited to thank you until I had them a little while, so that I can now share with you some of the joy I'm experiencing. I can't believe that now I can hear the phone ring from another room—even when there is some noise! I can't believe that now I can hear my children talk to me. . . . When I'm driving, I now can hear sirens. I can now hear small birds chirp. I feel more confident now in my job as a mother and also more relaxed. There are some sounds I hear but don't know what they are. I'm told, in time, my brain will start learning to put together things I've never heard before. Everyone is trying to learn how to talk quieter to me. Seems we sure live in a noisy world!

There is no price you can put on the joy of hearing, Mr. Ross. I can never thank you enough for what you have done for me and my family. Thanks a million.

J. S.
Seattle, WA

There is no price you can put on sincere "thank you's" either. Gratitude is a precious reward, the treasured gift sought by all.

A "thank you" costs little; give it, always.

SAY "I'M SORRY"

Saying you're sorry is a powerful way of showing respect; and sometimes you must say you're sorry if you expect people to come to your aid.

Often the reason people need help is that they've made a mistake and gotten themselves into a jam. If you're in that situation, your best bet—if you want assistance—is to admit the error of your ways. People like to help people who show a willingness to reform.

I'm always willing to listen when people tell me they're sorry. A fifteen-year-old Illinois girl got herself pregnant, dropped out of high school, and gave birth to a baby girl. The young lady had no source of income, her father was out of work, and there was scarcely enough money for milk and food for the baby. There are many, many unwed teenage mothers in this country, and I can't begin to help them all. This young woman caught my attention. Here, in part, is the letter she wrote to me:

Dear Mr. Ross,

Mom and Dad were always telling me I was too young to go steady. I thought I was pretty cool and knew it all. What a joke! It's too late now, but I really wish I had listened to them. . . .

Mom has offered to help with Lisa if I find a job. . . . By phone, I've been answering household-help ads. I even offer to scrub floors but no one will consider me unless I apply in person. . . .

I need some decent clothes so I can apply for jobs. Mr. Ross, could you spare $85 for me to buy a new dress, a pair of shoes, and some pantyhose? Another $15 for bus fares would be real helpful.

I need a new start, Mr. Ross. I really love my baby and will do anything so I don't have to give her up. . . .

R. A.
Chicago, Illinois

Here was my reply:

Dear Miss R. A.,

I'm your friend and won't desert you. You deserve a new start. I also don't believe that moralizing about your situation will help any.

What's done is done. Let's keep looking ahead. With your attitude, I assure you . . . everything will turn out for the best.

My $200 check is enclosed for some new clothes and bus fares. The other $25 is to buy something nice for Lisa.

To err is human; all of us do the wrong thing at times. All of us need to say we're sorry many, many times during our lives. When you make a mistake, admit it. When you hurt someone, apologize. Don't insist you're right when you know in your heart you're wrong.

Some people, after they make mistakes, think the way to get others to help them is to pretend they did nothing wrong. It seldom works. Many business people make bad decisions and suffer financial reverses. Then, when seeking funds to recover, they blame the economy or competition for their troubles. Investors raise their eyebrows. In my experience, business people are more convincing if they say, "I did such and such wrong, and now I know I should do thus and so."

In any profession or situation, if you admit your mistakes immediately, others will more surely do as you wish. A New York advertising man created a direct-mail piece for a small publisher in New Jersey. In a test mailing, the piece didn't bring in enough sales to pay for itself. The publisher expected the advertising man to defend his piece, finding reasons why it "should have worked." But the advertising man simply said, "It didn't work. Now what I suggest we try is . . ." Impressed with the man's good sense and willingness to change, the publisher authorized a new direct-mail piece, which worked. Had the advertising man failed to acknowledge his failure, he could easily have lost his client.

Admit error; say you're sorry. You'll persuade people more often if you do.

Less effective:

- "We couldn't deliver on time because we didn't have enough lead time, and some of our people got sick. We'll do better the next time."
- "Don't blow your top; you only had to wait 20 minutes. The traffic was terrible and I got here as fast as I could. . . ."
- "Mom, why won't you let me start driving the car again? That accident wasn't my fault."

More effective:

- "I miscalculated the amount of lead time we'd need, and I didn't allow for the fact that some of our people might get sick. I'm sorry the shipment was late. I hope you'll give us another try. We'll do better next time; I promise."
- "I forgot how bad traffic can be this time of day. I'm sorry I kept you waiting."
- "Mom, I'm really sorry I bashed in that fender. I know how much you love your new car. If you'll let me drive again, I promise to be a lot more careful."

In addition to saying "please," "thank you," and "I'm sorry," you can show respect in two other important ways.

NEATNESS PAYS

Neatness—in letters, in dress, or in appearance—is important when you are making a request. Neatness scores points with most everybody.

When asking anyone for anything, don't blow your chances by neglecting your appearance. Appearances may not make the person, but it makes a difference. An amazing number of people neglect such basics. A carefully handwritten or typed letter makes a better impression than a carelessly prepared request. Smudges, words crossed out, coffee stains, and the like imply casualness and lack of respect for the other person.

One day in 1958, a young man named Ted Aaron showed up at my factory in Eau Claire, Wisconsin. He was clean and neat, dressed in blue jeans, a work shirt, and well-polished shoes. "I'm looking for work," Ted said. I looked him over and liked what I saw; but I really didn't need more help. "What can you do?" I asked. "I'll do anything," he said. "Anything's better than welfare." I asked if he was willing to clean up the place. He said sure, and I hired him on the spot.

I didn't have to tell him what to do. If he saw a piece of paper on the floor, he picked it up. If he saw grease on a machine, he cleaned it off. And he didn't have to ask where the cleaning fluid was; he just found it.

I was delighted. Here was a man who—in appearance and performance—lived up to my ideal of neatness. He also had a great concern for detail; and he willingly took on more important jobs in the company. Over the years he rose from assistant janitor to general manager. Later he became vice president of another company, and retired a wealthy man. While his neatness may not have been the key to his success, it was an accurate clue to his attention to detail in every aspect of his life.

LIVE UP TO PROMISES

Most of the bank loans in this country are made to people who took out loans previously—and paid them back on schedule. Usually you take on some sort of obligation every time you ask for something, whether it's money, a favor, or whatever. Live up to that obligation; doing so qualifies you to ask again and receive in the future. It shows that you respect yourself—and the person or institution you have accepted an obligation from. .

Let me give you an example of what I mean by living up to your promises and obligations. Many years ago, before I became wealthy, I had saved up enough money to buy my wife, Laurian, a mink coat. She wore it once when we got together with five couples who were very good friends of ours. The wives oh'd and ah'd over the mink, and in a flood of good feeling, I said jokingly, "Some day, when I make it big, I'll buy one for each of you."

Well, they never let me forget it. Over the years they kept reminding me. They kidded me with statements like, "It doesn't have to be street-length, Percy, just a jacket will do." Every few months, they escalated their needling:

"How about just a mink collar, Percy, or a scarf?"

"If you can't make it mink coats, how about a few handbags of red squirrel?"

"How about just giving us a couple of minks, and we'll breed our own?"

"Just buy us a hunting license, Percy, and we'll trap our own mink."

It was all in good fun, and I don't think they really expected me to come through, but as I later told a newspaper columnist, "A promise is a promise, whether it's spoken or in writing."

When I sold my plastic company, Poly-Tech, I had finally made it big. The ladies would have their mink coats! I rented the entire Standard Club dining room and arranged for Roy Bjorkman (a local furrier) to show about a hundred of his finest mink coats.

I invited the five couples to dinner, keeping the minks a secret. Between tenderloin steaks and champagne, I reminisced a bit about what I had promised fourteen years earlier. As the musicians played "Promises, Promises," the curtain parted and six of Minneapolis's top models strolled down the runway, showing the selection of coats. I then announced, "Ladies, take your pick. There's a mink for each of you!"

I was able to fulfill my promise because I achieved success. But the opposite is also true: I became successful because I always took my promises seriously. If you want to succeed at anything, be a person of your word. It gives you the strength to take your own self seriously, and that strength gets other people behind you.

SHOW RESPECT EVERY WAY YOU CAN

There are many, many ways to show your regard for people. Here are a few.

Put on a happy face. You're not fully dressed without a smile. A sour expression seldom invites a "yes." Why do you think President Reagan gets his way so often? One of his biggest pluses, I think, is that wonderful, radiant smile of his. Who can resist it?

Communicate confidence with your body. Stand straight and tall. Give a firm, positive handshake. I often teach young children how to shake hands. I tell them a firm handshake is much more impressive than a weak one.

Create a "comfort zone." Start with pleasant small talk. Ask other people about their families, work, and hobbies. Get to know them, and develop a genuine interest in them. I've found that I influence people better if I first warm them up this way. Once I offered a silver dollar to a young boy in an amusement park. The boy's mother pulled him away and said, "Don't talk to strangers!" My mistake was failing to create a comfort zone. Without one, I couldn't even give away a silver dollar!

Respect the other person's time. When you request an appointment, few things make a poorer impression than being late. Just as the early bird catches the worm, the person who is on time gets the yes. And once your meeting is underway, get to the point quickly, and don't overstay your welcome—whether in person or on the telephone.

Don't contradict people. Few actions show disrespect more than telling people they're wrong. Find a positive way to press your point. For example, when people say they're too busy to see you, don't reply, "But you could make time if you wanted to." Instead say, "I know what that's like." Then approach them from a different angle.

Make people feel important. Lewis E. Lawes, former warden of Sing Sing, could get his way with just about anyone. When asked his secret for handling a hardened criminal, he said, "There is only one possible way of getting the better of him—treat him as if he were an honorable gentleman." People seldom say "yes" to those who make them feel small. Build people up if you want them on your side.

THE PERCY ROSS IMPROVEMENT PLAN FOR SHOWING RESPECT: THE BEST PEOPLE DO IT

During the next few days, try showing more respect to people. I think you'll be delighted at the way they respond. Follow these steps:

1. Write down several things you plan to ask for in the near future.

2. Decide on the best way to show more respect when you ask for these things. For each item on your list, consider which of the following approaches is best:

- Saying "please"
- Saying "thank you"
- Saying "I'm sorry"
- Improving your neatness
- Living up to promises

For example, if you want to get a coworker to stop smoking in your work area, you might figure out a thoughtful way to say "please." And you might thank the person in advance for his or her trouble.

Show more respect whenever you can, however you can. Make it a habit from now on. You'll get more yeses if you do; and you'll also get more respect in return.

Chapter 11

An Obvious
Yet Neglected
Thing to Do

The class of 1934 at Calumet High in Calumet, Michigan, was holding its thirty-fourth annual reunion. I was rubbing elbows with friends and acquaintances I had not seen in years. At such events I like to reminisce about the good old days. But I couldn't help thinking—with a tug at my heart about opportunities missed—of the things that could have been if only I had done something differently, or acted instead of keeping quiet.

Dorothy Klapperich Chopp was standing nearby. I had had a crush on Dorothy back in high school. I thought she was great. So did all the other boys. But I never approached her. I worked every day after school to help our family, so I didn't have much time to make many friends. Besides, I was shy.

At the reunion, we caught each other's eye and smiled. *What the heck*, I thought, *I'll say it.*

"Dorothy, I used to want to date you," I said as offhandedly as I could, "but you were always taken."

Dorothy smiled broadly and said, "You should have tried harder."

I should have asked her out, she was saying. I had been afraid to try, afraid she'd say no. Even if she had, I should have asked, and kept on asking. I hadn't applied my father's advice.

Too many people, like me back then, shrink from asking. Or if they ask, and are turned down, they give up. In order to get anything in this life—a date, a raise, cooperation, a million dollars, absolutely anything—you've got to apply my ninth rule for success:

- **Rule #9**   *Ask . . . And Keep Asking.*

Let me give you another example of what I mean. Back in 1951, I couldn't pay a note that was due at the bank. I was short on cash for groceries, and my wife and I had two small sons to feed. I asked all my friends for a loan to tide us over, but they all turned me down. I asked business associates, everybody I could think of. They all said no; they thought I was washed up, I guess. The future looked pretty bleak. If I had stopped asking for help then, life *could* have been bleak. But I didn't stop. Instead, I asked again.

Something told me that I should approach Kid Cann. I didn't know the man, I had only read about him in the newspapers. He was involved, they said, in various types of illegal and questionable deals.

When I met Cann at the office of his local night club, I was scared. My palms were sweating. I don't remember all I said. I blurted out my situation—being broke and not able to provide for my wife and two children. I looked him in the eyes and said, "Will you please lend me $500? I'll pay you back as soon as possible." He gave me the money, in cash, and said, "Don't worry about it, young man. Pay me back whenever you can."

About a year later, he sounded surprised when I phoned for another appointment. We met the next evening at his night club, but it was Cann who really surprised me. As I was handing him back the money I'd borrowed, he shook his head, smiled broadly, and said, "Percy, you keep it. Pass the favor on to someone else who's in need someday."

Kid Cann had compassion for others. When he died years later, I went to his funeral and couldn't help but wonder how many others he had helped.

Asking makes things happen. If you want to get anything, accomplish anything, or enjoy anything, you've got to communicate your needs. It's not enough to know what you want (Rule #1), to pick the right person to ask (Rule #2), to prepare a good case for yourself (Rule #3), to put giving into your asking (Rule #4), and to apply the other rules I've mentioned. You must bite the bullet and *ask*!

FAILURE STEMS FROM NOT ASKING

Perhaps you've heard the following story, or another like it. A certain salesman was hoping to get an order from a toy company for many truckloads of wood; but he lost out to a competitor. The man was particularly upset because he had gone to great pains to court the toy company's president.

One day he worked up the courage to ask for an explanation. "Bob, I'm puzzled. How come you bought that wood from Apex? You and I belong to the same club; we've been playing golf together for months; we've had lunch together dozens of times. Why didn't you place an order with *me*?"

The president stroked his chin, then replied: "Larry, you never *asked*."

Sales managers tell lots of stories like this because so many of their representatives—who must live by asking—fail to ask for orders!

If something is to happen, you need to ask. Many business people and employees—all types of people, in fact—shortchange themselves by failing to *ask* for what they need.

An executive I know promoted one of two equally qualified managers to the post of research director. I asked him how he made his selection. Three years ago, he explained, the man who got the job took him aside and told him, "I want to head up research and development some day."

"I never forgot that," said the executive. The other fellow may have wanted the position just as badly, but he didn't let the president know it.

Some parents complain that their children never mow the lawn, clean their rooms, or take out the garbage. Many of these parents have never taken their children aside, looked them in the eye, and said clearly and firmly—but without threat or resentment—what they want done.

Disappointment, regret, resentment, and failure often stem from the same root: inaction. More often than not, that inaction is characterized by *not asking*. Such people are not taking the steps to get others behind them. Other people are the source of your success and happiness; they will gladly help you get where you want to go. But they can't read your mind. The secret of getting what you want out of life is so simple: Let others know your needs; request their help in making your dreams come true.

If you aren't getting all you want out of life, if you're not advancing in your career fast enough to suit you, if you're not making the money you want, if your human relationships are not as rich and rewarding as you'd like, then you're not asking persistently enough.

To turn things around—to enrich your life immeasurably—you need only apply Rule #9.

SUCCESS STARTS WITH ASKING FOR WHAT YOU WANT

Henry Ford once asked a friend to lend him $10,000. He was given the money, and with it he started the Ford Motor Company. What if Ford had been too shy to ask?

Steve Jobs and Steve Wosniac had no assets or cash, but they wanted to build and sell small computers for hobbyists. So Jobs asked three electronics distributors to give them parts worth $25,000. He promised to pay them for the parts within 30 days. Think of it—a kid with no money asking for $25,000 worth of merchandise on trust! Jobs and Wosniac made 100 computers practically overnight, sold them, and paid the distributors 29 days later. This was the start of Apple Computer and the personal computer revolution. What if Steve Jobs hadn't found the courage to ask?

If you don't ask, nothing happens. It is only when you ask that something can happen. This is true for inventors and industrialists, teachers and writers, clerks and policemen, children and adults.

If you're a parent and you want your son or daughter to do something, *ask*. When my father asked me to sell eggs door-to-door, I did, even though it meant I couldn't play much with other children—because I wanted to help my family.

If you're a manager and you want a certain level of performance from employees, ask them for it. Some time back, a man I know who publishes newsletters was disturbed by the fact that each of his editors wrote just two articles a week. He knew they could do more; and greater output would allow the company to buy fewer articles from freelancers. He hinted to the editors that they ought to increase their output, tried "motivational" techniques, but nothing seemed to work. The editors continued to produce just two articles a week each. Then it dawned on the publisher that he had never really asked for what he wanted. So he called a meeting and said, "I want each of you to start producing three articles a week, and I want them to be first-rate. This will be the new standard. I know you can do it. If you need any help or advice, I'm here."

The editors grumbled a bit, but came through with flying colors. Within two months, they were each producing three excellent articles a week.

Look into the life of anyone who has succeeded, and I guarantee you will find a long history of asking "no matter what." Let me give you an example from a letter I received as a result of my column:

Dear Mr. Ross,

Hi, my name is Jodi. I'm 13 and live in a small town.

Each year I raise money for Muscular Dystrophy. Last year I took in $702 by saving aluminum cans, selling raffle tickets, skating in a skate-a-thon. I spend most of my summers working to raise money for M.D.A.

This year I set my goal at $1,000 and I'm running short. I have so far raised $375. There won't be a skate-a-thon this year, so I have been doing all I can to bring in money in other ways.

Could you help me by coming to Sturgeon Lake and have an auction? I will ask all the business places to donate things if you will auction them off.

J. S.
Sturgeon Lake, Minnesota

How could I resist? I wrote back:

Dear Jodi,

"Going once! Going twice! Going three times! SOLD!" Count on me to be your auctioneer. I will also bring a 19″ RCA color TV for the auction. We'll try to reach your goal.

Needless to say, she raised more than the $1,000. This was a young lady who really knew how to pop the question. I learned later that Jodi had been asking for money for muscular dystrophy for several years.

She can't explain why; she doesn't know anyone with muscular dystrophy, but she once told a newspaper reporter, "I'd love to see the people in wheelchairs be able to get up and skate." At age seven, she sold popcorn, pens, and zucchinis for M.D.A. in front of her house. In an interview with the *Duluth News-Tribune & Herald*, her mother was quoted as saying, "She put the picnic table out in the street, almost blocking traffic, and screamed, 'Zucchinis for MDA!'" With asking skills like that, the young lady is bound to become anything she wants.

Be like Jodi. Put your table in the street, and shout if you have to.

KEEP ON ASKING

What if you ask and get turned down?

As I've said already, time after time my father used to say to me, "Percy, don't give up, don't ever give up." You've got to apply the second part of Rule #9: *Keep on asking.*

Persistence pays. If you want results, keep asking until you get them. *If you don't get results the first time you ask, then ask again, and again.*

Some people think successful people, especially the rich, get what they want without much effort. It isn't so. I had to ask again and again for help when I was poor, and once I became rich, I *still* had to keep asking.

Everybody who succeeds at anything has to ask—often repeatedly—for help of some sort. That's par for the course; it's the nature of the game. Those who think otherwise need to open their eyes.

Elias Howe, inventor of the sewing machine, didn't have enough money to build his brainchild when he was starting out. He looked far and wide for an investor, and was turned down repeatedly. Instead of giving up, he approached a boyhood friend, who gave him $500. That was all he needed to get started.

Admiral Hyman Rickover was also persistent. His original proposal for a nuclear submarine was shelved by the Navy. The project was as good as dead. But Rickover refused to take no for an answer.

He went to Admiral Nimitz, got him to agree that an atomic sub—if one could be built—would be "militarily desirable." This admission got Rickover into the Atomic Energy Commission. The scientists there agreed that a nuclear-powered engine was practical, and issued a statement to that effect.

Then Rickover, with his new backing, revised his original proposal and took it to the Joint Chiefs of Staff. This time it wasn't shelved. Five years and $40 million later, the *Nautilus*, the first atomic submarine, was a sleek reality.

After Steve Jobs and Steve Wosniac sold their first 100 homemade computers, they thought they had the makings of a successful company. Steve Jobs went to Regis McKenna, head of the prestigious advertising company of the same name, and asked him to represent Apple. Of course Jobs had no money to offer. McKenna said no. He went back a second time. McKenna said no again. Steve went back a third time. McKenna still said no.

What did Jobs do next? He went back a fourth time! Here is what he said, as reported in *Penthouse* magazine: "Regis, I have no money to pay you. I want you to do our ads. We're going to be an incredibly successful computer company. Trust me. Just trust me. I'll pay you in a year."

Steve looked McKenna right in the eye (that's important). Finally McKenna said, "Okay."

Persistence *does* pay. It impresses people with the seriousness of your intent. You've got to keep coming back, you've got to keep asking. The other day I read about a young man named Craig Vetter, the fellow who invented the plastic windshield for motorcycles. Not one manufacturer took his invention seriously. He tried them all. No dice. But he didn't give up. He asked his girlfriend for money. She lent him all of $83, and he started his own company. By 1978, when he sold out, he was taking in $16 million a year.

I could give you endless examples of people who asked and asked and asked, then asked *one more time*—and succeeded.

Asking is powerful. It can work magic. I don't say asking is easy. It's not, and it doesn't work every time. But it does work if you persist. Harriet Beecher Stowe, an author I much admire, gives this advice: "When you get into a tight place and everything goes against you, till it seems as though you could not hold on a minute longer, never give up then, for that is just the place and the time that the tide will turn."

My father would say, "Amen."

TEST YOUR WILLINGNESS TO ASK

How good are you at asking . . . and asking again? Consider the following situation. It is based on a real-life story.

Suppose you are a young man living with your wife

in Washington, D.C. You're ready to start a family, and you very much want a home of your own. But your savings are small, and you earn only a modest salary as a reporter for a local newspaper. You have always admired the work of a certain famous architect, and you frequently daydream about living in a home designed especially for you by this man.

One day the crazy idea enters your head to write to the architect, asking him to create your dream house. He is known as the designer of expensive homes for wealthy people. Would *you* actually write to him?

A "no" answer would seem to be the most sensible. You haven't got enough money even to buy a modestly priced house, let alone build your dream home. Besides, wouldn't approaching this particular architect violate Rule #2 (Ask the Right Person)?

A conservative approach would be to save your money over a period of years, then put a down payment on an older home, or to seek the services of a "budget" architect.

If you answered "yes," you are probably more of a risk-taker. Writing to the architect, explaining your situation, you stand an excellent chance of getting turned down flat.

Suppose, however, a miracle happens: You ask— and he agrees to design your home! Now you've got a problem. Where will you get the money for his fee, construction, and land? You go to your bank and request a loan. They practically laugh in your face. What do you do next?

1. Write the architect explaining you are unable to finance a home, at least at the present time.
2. Try another lending institution.

Many people would write the architect, sighing with disappointment and resignation. Suppose, however, you apply for a loan at another lending institution, and another, and another. They all say no. What would you do now?

1. Gracefully admit defeat; write the architect.
2. Search for other ways to raise the money.

Sometimes, when you've been turned down repeatedly, the sensible thing is to stop. You're just beating your head against a brick wall; the effort isn't worth it. Other times, if you *really want* what you're asking for, it is worth it to *ask one more time* or *ask one more person*. Such determination is what separates success from failure.

What happened in this real-life situation? Loren Pope, back in the 1930s, dreamed of living in a home designed by Frank Lloyd Wright, one of the most skilled and respected architects of all time. Pope, a $50-a-week news editor for the *Washington Evening Star*, could hardly afford luxurious living. But he took pen in hand and wrote Wright, asking him to design a home for himself and his wife. Mr. Wright's terse reply came back, "Of course I am ready to give you a house."

Ecstatic, Pope sought a building loan from a local lending institution, was turned down, then went to another and another. They all said no. Finally, in desperation, he approached his employers. They advanced him $5,700, to be repaid in weekly installments of $12.

Wright designed a classic but affordable structure, based on principles he called "Usonian"; and in early

1941 the delighted couple moved in. Today the Pope-Leighey House, as it is now known, is open to the public as a museum operated by the National Trust for Historical Preservation.

THE PERCY ROSS IMPROVEMENT PLAN FOR LEARNING AN OBVIOUS YET NEGLECTED THING TO DO

If you want to apply Rule #9 more aggressively, consider these three suggestions:

1. Start by asking for more little things. Ask for a favor, a stick of gum, the time of day, anything. Ask for several small things. Practice asking, and make it a habit. In particular, ask for things you may now hesitate to ask for.

- "Waiter, may we have a booth instead of a table?"
- "Marilyn, if you would check with me each time before sending out the invoices, I'd appreciate it."
- "Adam, we're in a bind. Can you work until 6:30 tonight?"
- "We'd like to take advantage of the quantity discount, but we don't have the warehouse space. Could you store some of the stock for us?"

If, like me and millions of others, you are reluctant to ask for intangible things—emotional support, consideration, or human courtesies—make a special point of requesting such things during the next few days:

- "Rachel, you said something this morning that upset me. Could we talk about it?"
- "Michael, you're interrupting! Let me finish my point; then the floor is yours. Okay?"

2. Take a chance; ask for something big! Most of us have a tendency to shy away from the very things we most want. We put off asking for them because we're afraid of getting turned down.

What is it your heart desires? What do you dream about? Who could give it to you, or help you make it come true? Go ahead, *ask them*!

- "Jane, will you marry me?"
- "I'd like you to invest in my new company. Will you?"
- "J. B., I want to become a supervisor. Will you consider me when a spot opens up?"
- "I'd like our company to be your main supplier. If I prepare a proposal, will you arrange a meeting with your president?"

If you find that you stop short of going for the gold, then prepare yourself to ask for it by using visualization. Mentally rehearse the proposal to Jane; imagine approaching your boss about that promotion. If negative thoughts or doubts creep into your mind, push them out.

Keep your imaging upbeat and positive. Run through your approach constructively and realistically. Work out the bugs, confront your fears—psych yourself up. Then start dialing Jane's number; knock on your boss's door. Get ready, get set, *ask*!

3. Think of something you once wanted but stopped asking for. Plan to ask again. Maybe you've asked two or three times—then caved in. Take your dream, project, or objective off ice and *ask one more time.*

- "Mr. Jensen, we'd really like a home of our own. I'm working full-time now, and I think I'm a good risk. Would you reconsider our mortgage application?"
- "Ladies and gentlemen: You might ask, how can a three-time loser be thick-headed enough to run for mayor yet again? I love this town, and there are things about it that need changing."
- "Henry, I haven't brought this up for a long time because it's as painful to me as it is to you. He's your son. You can't keep on hating him. Please call him."
- "Dear Ms. Harmon: I think your company is pretty special; that's why I'm writing again. Could we meet, whether or not you currently have an opening?"

Decide what you really want; pick the right person to approach; prepare a good case for yourself. Then take the great leap. *Ask . . . and keep asking.* Do this and anything is possible.

Chapter 12

Don't Be
an Island

At the beginning of this book, I invited you to ask for the moon. You *can* have the moon; in fact, you can have anything you want. But first you'll need to apply Rule #10. You'll hear more yeses if you apply it; you'll benefit in deeper ways as well.

What is Rule #10? It is a spiritual magnet for bringing things together, a force that can unify families, groups, communities, and nations:

- **Rule #10   Go Beyond "Me" to "We."**

Like many of the other rules of asking, Rule #10 is deceptively simple—yet it packs an enormous wallop. If practiced on a wide scale, it can transform your life.

What does "Go Beyond 'Me' to 'We'" mean? When you ask for something, go beyond yourself; help the person you're asking to go beyond him or herself too. Include other people in your dreams and desires. Poet

John Donne wrote, "No man is an island, entire of itself; every man is a piece of the continent, a part of the main . . ."

People who violate Rule #10 lock themselves into the psychology of me–you, have–have not, win–lose. The trouble with life today, the source of discord in the world, is the me-against-you attitude that pits group against group, class against class, race against race, nation against nation. Asking, if done with Rule #10 in mind, helps to bridge that separation. It gives you and the other person an opportunity to depend on and support one another, to join hands and hearts, to share, to make both sides winners.

GENUINE FEELING

Let me clarify Rule #10 with a few examples. Some time ago a sixty-eight-year-old farmer near La Crosse, Wisconsin, wrote me the following letter:

Dear Mr. Ross,

Doing OK at 68. Manage my small farm of 10 acres. Mostly chickens and a few hogs. Been living alone since my Mrs. died 11 years ago. Still miss her. Never wanted another woman. No kids.

Manage to keep house and do chores 'cause can't afford help. Too expensive. Make my own eats. Sold my '61 Ford pickup 5 years ago. Couldn't drive any more. Very good neighbors bring my feed and supplies from town. They even deliver my eggs to market.

No bad habits. Don't smoke. Don't drink—except coffee. Only complaint is my old Muntz TV set. Hasn't worked for a year. Can't get parts. Can't afford a new set. If you have a used black-and-white TV you can spare—would appreciate. If you haven't don't worry 'cause I've got a small radio. My best friend since the old Muntz went kaput.

Don't mind daytimes 'cause I keep busy. Nights are long and pretty lonely. Read about doings every week from my neighbor's *La Crosse Tribune*. Sorry for long letter. First time I wrote since my Mrs. died. I feel better now. Hope you live a long time.

W. H.
La Crosse, Wisconsin

I replied:

I remember "Mad Man" Muntz from the early days of TV. His company is no longer around. Expect a knock on your door soon. It'll be "Mad Man" Ross with a color TV for your loneliness. Have the coffee pot on and we'll swap stories about the old days.

Since he lived only 150 miles from my home in Minneapolis, I drove out and personally delivered the TV set. We had a great time gabbing about the way things used to be, consuming good hot coffee and fresh rolls.

His letter got through to me, and we hit it off in

person. "We"—that was the asking psychology. Together we *shared;* I felt we both benefited.

Consider, by contrast, this letter:

Dear Mr. Ross,

I am a 13-year-old girl. Mom is divorced and works to raise my two younger brothers and me. It's really impossible for me to save any money for extra clothes from the allowance I get.

I'm going on a trip to Florida to visit my really best girlfriend. So I really need $500 for new clothes, which my Mom won't buy me. You give to the really needy, and I really need new clothes for my trip. A check for $500 will really make me happy.

R. R.
Knoxville, Tennessee

Bearing Rule #10 in mind—"Go Beyond 'Me' to 'We'"—how do you think I reacted? Do you think I wrote out a $500 check? Do you think it would have been an act of true sharing? Would she and I have come together in common purpose and understanding? Here in fact is how I answered this young girl's letter:

Dear R.,

You said your mom *won't* buy you extra clothes . . . you didn't say *couldn't*. Mom *really* knows best.

NOT GETTING BUT SHARING

The best way to apply Rule #10 is to cultivate the spirit of sharing. It also helps to use the words "we," "us," and "our." Ration your use of "I," "me," "you," and "your." For example:

Less effective: "I want those invoices out by noon. Would you give Mary the figures she needs right away?"

More effective: "We need to get those invoices out by noon. How soon could you give Mary the figures she needs?"

Your attitude is the most important thing. If you put the "we" feeling into your heart as well as into your words, no matter what you ask for, others will be more likely to cooperate.

A story that drives home this point is one that Dale Carnegie used to tell (there's a version of it in *How to Win Friends and Influence People*). Years ago Bethlehem Steel paid Charles Schwab, its dynamic president, a salary of $1 million a year. This was back in the days when a million went a long way. Schwab earned his pay because he knew how to get results from people.

One day, the story goes, he came upon three of his workers smoking, in violation of company regulations. He had every right to reprimand them with the warning, "No smoking, men. You know the rules." But Schwab knew that such words violated the "we" spirit; they would only make the workers feel small and resistant. Instead, he simply reached into a pocket, took out three cigars, and gave one to each, saying, "Boys, have a cigar on me. But I would appreciate it if you would not smoke it during working hours."

Someone once asked Schwab how he came to have such loyal, hard-working employees. "I never criticize anyone," he explained. "The way to develop the best that is in a person is by appreciation and encouragement." He knew how to ask.

Suppose you're a salesperson getting ready to ask for the order. Here's an example of putting the "we" spirit into asking.

Less effective: "This Acme machine you're using, it's not the best, you know. Take a good look at our Apex. It's the best available." (Implication: You were a dummy to buy an Acme. I, however, am smart. Let me wise you up.)

More effective: "I'm sure you considered all the features and benefits when you bought your Acme. I know you're busy, but I hope you'll give the same consideration now to the Apex. I think you'll agree it's one heck of a machine." (Implication: You were smart back then, and I'm sure you'll be smart now. Let's do business together.)

173

Suppose you're a parent and you want your child to spend more time practicing the piano. Remember that "we" spirit of asking.

Less effective: "You're wasting my hard-earned money, and I hate nagging you about this all the time."
(Implication: You aren't being very nice to me. You are causing discord in the family.)

More effective: "I love to hear you play. You could get to be very good at it; you just need to practice more."
(Implication: You could be the greatest; I'm behind you.)

Go beyond "me" to "we" in everything you ask for—money or assistance, goods or cooperation.

TAKING POSSESSION

Rule #10 is closely related to the two things people strive for so doggedly—*money* and *possessions.*

Let's look at possessions first. Rule #10 is intimately tied up with ownership, though this may not be obvious at first.

Let's say you own land. Does owning it give you the right to order people off your land, rifle in hand, as they do in Westerns? I don't think so, not ultimately. True ownership does not, to me, imply separation from the rest of the community, but rather a joining in with the community. Ownership *does* involve rights, including the right of exclusive use, but it means—or should mean—something deeper as well.

I know a man who owns a 200-acre suburban estate, complete with mansion, riding trails, and nine-hole golf course. The trouble is, he's constantly away on business; and when he's home, he's preoccupied. Who really "owns" the place—the man or his gardener?

Nobody really "owns" anything in this world, except through enjoyment of it. And enjoyment is usually increased by sharing. What good is a boat, for example, if there isn't someone with you to sail in it? Money too, I have found, can be pretty useless unless you share it.

True ownership is possible only for those with the capacity to appreciate and enjoy what they own. This is true of anything—land, cars, houses, paintings, pets, gardens, a record collection. It's also true of people. You may say that your wife, husband, child, or friend is "yours." I hope this is richly so. The other person is "yours" to the extent that there is perception, acceptance, appreciation, and a relaxed state of "being together."

The "we" spirit is always part of true ownership. When you hog or hoard, you do not truly possess or own—in any sense of the word. Only through the joy of give and take is anything yours. I have found this to be true of my own possessions—especially of my money.

A young lady once asked me if wealth made me happy. I replied, "No, but *sharing* it does."

Go beyond "me" to "we." Share what you have. Do this and you will truly appreciate what you have all the more—because the spirit of sharing will enrich your life.

THE ROOT OF ALL GOOD!

How does Rule #10 apply to money? First, we must understand what money is. Metal, paper, ink—in essence, nothing! Money is only as valuable as we make it.

One of Thoreau's friends, Ralph Waldo Emerson, put it well. "The value of a dollar," he said, "is social, as it is created by society."

Money is a social invention. Why did our ancestors invent it? To simplify trading—the transfer of food-stuffs, clothing, tools, specialized skills. Being light and portable, it could be exchanged in lieu of items that were bulky, distant, complicated, abstract, or promised in the future. Money is an implement of trading or transfer—in other words, *money is a tool that allows people to share*. It is worthless by itself. Here is a letter from a reader of my column. I think it illustrates very well what I mean:

Dear Mr. Ross,

I like reading your column. You must really enjoy spreading your money around to help others during your lifetime. I congratulate you.

Most rich people never stop trying to accumulate more and more money. Some must even think they can take it with them when they go.

How do you explain what you are doing in contrast to many other rich people who just keep piling it up?

L. K.
St. Louis, Missouri

Here was my reply:

Dear Mrs. K.,

Money is like fertilizer. In a pile it helps nothing grow. Spread it around . . . it works miracles.

If you have the wrong idea about money—if you think it's worth anything on its own, or if you think it's a tool for "getting" things—then you're in for trouble. The truest purpose of money is for the promotion of sharing and caring. Money can be the root of all good *if* you know what it is and how to use it.

When you ask for money and violate Rule #10, you show only selfishness. Consider this letter from a California woman:

Dear Mr. Ross,

Since you're being so darn generous I am not at all embarrassed as I ask for the following: a farm in the country, Rolls-Royce, yacht (150-foot), Swiss bank account of five figures, wardrobe from Saks, and a motorbike.

Being a millionaire, you can easily afford my dream list.

S. U.
Santa Ana, California

My reply:

Dear S.,

Your list is too big for me. I'm a millionaire, not a billionaire. Try Santa Claus.

People respond to askers who show a caring, sharing spirit. Whenever you ask for anything, especially money, take care not to treat the other person as an "island." Treat the other person as "part of the main"—a person joined with you in spirit.

Someone who makes a request while getting across the idea of "we" instead of "me" has a much better chance of succeeding. Consider the following three requests. If you were the boss, which would impress you most?

Request #1: "Boss, things are tight at home. Food costs more these days; property taxes just went up; my daughter wants to take skiing lessons. . . . I hate to bring it up, and I hope I'm not out of line, but do you think maybe we could talk about a small raise?"

Request #2: "Boss, I'm upset about something, and I'd better get it off my chest. A year ago, I was turning out a widget a day. Now I'm doing a widget and a half. But my salary hasn't changed. My wife has been bugging me; she thinks it isn't right that I haven't got a raise.

I'm doing more, so I should be worth more. I'm making $300 now. Shouldn't I be making $450?"

Request #3: "Boss, you remember a year ago, I could only turn out one widget a day. You gave me some pointers, and now I'm doing a widget and a half a day. I'm shooting for two widgets a day. I think I'm doing a good job; I'd really like to make a contribution to this company. I like working here and I'm willing to give it my all. Would you please consider giving me a small raise now? Eventually, I'd hope some day to get into supervision and work up to a really good salary."

If you were the boss, wouldn't you go for Request #3? In Request #1, the person says he needs more pay, but he doesn't point out that he is *worth* more. He hasn't taken his request far enough—the "we" spirit is missing.

In Request #2, the person points out that he is producing more and deserves a raise. But his request bristles with "me." Note the tone of accusation in "But my salary hasn't changed."

In Request #3, like #2, the person points out that he has become more productive and therefore more deserving of a raise. Yet he also creates a meeting of the minds when he says "You gave me some pointers . . ." He further builds the "we" feeling by saying he likes his work and wants to contribute more and move ahead.

I think I've made my point. Ask for money, ask for anything, but ask in the spirit of "we." Plan to create mutual satisfaction and growth. Ask for the power to do that.

IF YOU HAVE FAITH, YOU'RE NOT ALONE

If you want to apply Rule #10 wholeheartedly, it is my belief that you must call upon the Almighty.

I began drawing on this power many years ago. After one of my business failures, I felt worthless, friendless, and depressed. Somehow I kept going, but it cost me a heart attack. I came close to dying. The doctor gave me only a few years to live unless I slowed down. As I lay in my hospital bed, I began thinking, questioning, and searching. In my own way, I prayed. I said, "I won't give up. I want to live." I would accept death, if that was my fate, but I asked for an extension—and got it.

Five years later, far from being dead, I was fit as a fiddle. Now I say "thank you" for my life many times a day.

Go beyond "me" to "we." Write Rule #10 in your heart.

THE PERCY ROSS IMPROVEMENT PLAN FOR GOING BEYOND "ME" TO "WE": DON'T BE AN ISLAND

If you feel you are asking from the isolated "island" of yourself, try asking as part of the common "continent" during the next few days. I think you'll find that others will respond more favorably to you.

1. List some things you plan to ask for in the near future. They could be small things, such as persuading a shop owner to exchange some merchandise, or larger things, such as convincing someone to be your partner in a business venture.

2. Review how you plan to ask. For each item on your list, imagine what you would say to the person. Rehearse your request in your mind. Then step back and decide whether the "me" spirit or the "we" spirit prevails.

For example, a woman who bought a coat on sale found when she got it home that it had a minor flaw in it. The store's policy was not to exchange sale items. She found herself mentally arguing with the managers, until she realized this approach would only put the manager off.

If necessary, rehearse a more positive way of asking, one that will make the other person feel you're both on the same wavelength. Go through your request in your mind a few times; make sure it's free of unkind words or negative implications.

3. Draw the other person to your side when you ask. Make your request positive, in the "we" spirit.

The woman who bought the coat went back to the store prepared to be friendly. Her plan was to say something pleasant to create a good mood, then to discuss the damaged coat in a reasonable way. She noticed a ring on the manager's finger and said, "That's onyx, isn't it?"

"Yes."

"Very pretty. I have a pair of onyx earrings."

They chatted for a couple of minutes, and when the atmosphere was right, the woman said, "I've got a problem. I know you don't ordinarily exchange sale items, but would you take a look at this . . ." The manager exchanged the coat without an argument.

During the next few days, make a point of getting people on your side before asking them for anything. You'll be more influential, and happier too.

Part III

GO AHEAD—
ASK FOR
THE MOON

Chapter 13

Set Up an
"Asking Program"

This chapter is for people who want to transform their lives. If you're serious about reaching ambitious goals—becoming president of a company, making it in the music business, raising beautiful kids, becoming happier, getting rich—and if you don't mind changing a few habits, read on.

If not, skip this chapter. You can still get enormous value from this book by reading the other chapters. The principles of asking will sink in automatically, and I think you'll find yourself getting what you want more often. However, if you want to *maximize* your results, you need a deliberate plan and special effort.

Still with me? Good!

Your life can be just about anything you want it to be. The sky's the limit! You can achieve your wildest goals. While not all desires will necessarily be satisfied, I am confident that your chances of reaching your goals are high.

Why do I feel this way? I know that lots of people

will be behind you; they are going to help make your dreams come true. These people are going to support you like an army of volunteers.

Who are these people, and why are they going to help you? They are your family, your friends, people you work with, schoolmates, shopkeepers, bankers, accountants, professional people of all types, even strangers and people you haven't even met yet. These people are going to do whatever it takes to make sure your deepest desires come true. They're going to, because you're going to ask them to. It's as simple as that.

Have you been going through life thinking you've got to make it on your own? Do you assume that success depends upon your individual efforts?

If so, I'm here to tell you it almost never happens that way. Success is usually a team effort; you're the star, coach, and cheerleader of your particular team. You should never think of yourself as a lone, individual competitor.

That's the point of this book. To get what you want in life, you've got to ask others for help. You're *supposed* to ask. You *owe* it to yourself to ask. Other people *want* you to ask; some are even *depending* upon you to ask.

Reach out, my friend. That's the secret of achieving anything good in life. When you do, you'll see yourself move closer to whatever goals you set your sights on.

The asking program I am going to suggest you follow to improve your skills consists of three simple steps: (1) Compile a list of things you want—large and small, short-term and long-term; (2) Figure out how to ask for those things; and (3) Ask for them!

STEP 1: CREATE A MASTER LIST OF THINGS YOU WANT

Make a master list of the things you want, and review it from time to time in the future. Two questionnaires will help you develop your list.

QUESTIONNAIRE A: LONG-TERM DESIRES

The following questions will help you "brainstorm" about your deepest needs. Get several sheets of blank paper or a note pad. Jot down whatever answers come to mind as you read each question. Later, look back at your answers. They will help you to develop your master list. (Don't feel you need to write something down for each question; make notes only when you feel inspired to do so.)

1. What do you wish you could achieve during your lifetime?

2. What single thing would make you most happy?

3. What do you daydream about most often?

4. Rank the following items, from 1 to 5, in the order of their importance to you:

   ( ) making lots of money
   ( ) being well-known or famous
   ( ) doing what you enjoy
   ( ) sharing friendship or love
   ( ) making a difference through your work

5. If you could become a famous person of a bygone era, who would it be? If you were that person, transported to the present time, what goals would you set for yourself?

6. In the future, if you had a chance to put your best abilities to use, what might you be doing?

7. Suppose, many years in the future, someone is making a speech about you at an awards ceremony. What does he or she say about your contributions at work or in your profession?

8. Suppose, when you are quite old, each of your children (if you have any) writes you a letter thanking you for your help, love, and guidance. What does each letter say?

9. In your work (or studies), how have you been most successful in the past? Think of two or three triumphs.

10. In your personal life, what are you most proud of? Think of two or three good things you have done.

11. What do you want very much but fear going after?

12. If you inherited $1 million, what would you do for the rest of your life?

13. If you could accomplish only one thing during the rest of your lifetime, what would it be?

14. What is your main goal in life?

15. What are some other important goals in your life?

QUESTIONNAIRE B: SHORT-TERM DESIRES

The following questions will help you think of some of the smaller things you want or need in the very near future. Jot down whatever answers come to mind as you read each question. (Again, make notes only when you feel inspired to do so.)

1. What do you want most right now?

2. What do you most need right now?

3. What would you most like to accomplish in the immediate future?

4. What do you want or need during the next 24 hours?

5. What do you want or need during the next few days?

6. What do you want or need during the next few weeks or months?

7. What do you want to own?

8. What do you wish you could experience or enjoy?

9. What do you want or need to get done right now?

10. Is anything bothering you right now? What do you wish could be done about it?

11. What do you want or need in the immediate future from each of the following people?

    • your spouse and/or friend
    • your mother and/or father
    • your children and/or grandchildren
    • your brothers and/or sisters
    • other relatives
    • close friends
    • acquaintances
    • people you work with
    • people you go to school with
    • people you know in your community and/or religious group
    • people in general

12. Is there anything you want or need from the following sources? What are those things?

    • doctor and/or dentist
    • accountant
    • lawyer
    • librarian or library
    • business consultant
    • specialist in science and/or engineering
    • career counselor
    • psychological counselor
    • minister, priest, or rabbi
    • public official and/or elected representative

13. What do you need now that you are not getting?

- mornings; afternoons; evenings
- weekends
- winter; spring; summer; fall
- holidays

14. Which of the following job-related items do you need?

   - a job
   - more satisfying work
   - more money
   - a business of your own
   - a decision on a career
   - preparation for a career
   - special education or training
   - a promotion
   - more responsibility
   - different work duties
   - more accomplishments on the job
   - recognition for your accomplishments
   - more enjoyment from work
   - better relations with your boss
   - better relations with your coworkers
   - better relations with customers or clients
   - the solution to a problem at work
   - the acceptance of an idea
   - information from someone
   - cooperation or a favor
   - less stress
   - time for a vacation or relaxation

15. Which of the following goals do you have for improving your health and fitness?

- lose or gain weight
- eat more nutritious foods
- get more exercise
- relax more
- have time for sports or recreation
- go dancing more often
- develop a physical skill or sport
- go on a vacation or trip
- get more sleep
- stop smoking
- cut down on drinking
- stop using drugs
- get sick less often
- improve your love life

16. What do you want in the way of money or wealth in the course of your life?

- a million dollars or more
- enough money to live a good life
- security for retirement
- ownership of stocks and bonds
- a bank loan or mortgage
- investment capital to finance a business venture

17. Which of the following possessions do you want?

- land, or more land
- a home of your own, or a better home
- landscaping, a garden, or a pool
- home improvements, or an addition to your home
- a place for an activity or hobby
- new furniture

- a washing machine, refrigerator, or other major appliance
- sports equipment or other recreational items
- a TV, stereo, VCR, computer, or other electronic equipment
- tools or implements
- a new wardrobe
- jewelry or furs
- a new car
- a boat or other recreational vehicle
- a bicycle, moped, or motorbike
- toys and games
- books, records, or cassettes
- paintings, sculptures, and other art works
- pets or livestock
- plants and other growing things
- other possessions

18. Which of the following entertainment and cultural activities would you like to enjoy more often?

- movies
- going to plays, concerts, the opera, and ballet
- going to rock concerts
- watching baseball, football, and other sports
- playing video games
- playing cards, chess, or other social games
- dining out
- going dancing
- visiting museums, galleries, or planetariums
- traveling or sightseeing
- reading books
- entertaining or going to parties

- cooking
- painting or sculpting
- singing or playing a musical instrument
- composing music
- writing poetry, fiction, or nonfiction
- acting
- studying a specialized field
- making or inventing things

19. In which of the following ways would you like to improve your personal relations?

- enjoy other people's company more
- get others to see the best in you
- see the best in others
- get someone to stop an annoying habit
- get the children to obey or do the right thing
- get parents to behave differently
- develop better communication with family members
- find new friends
- develop better communication with friends
- make someone like you better
- enjoy more affection with your spouse or loved one
- let people know you care about them
- find out what's bothering someone
- feel close to someone
- get others to follow your lead
- develop better teamwork or cooperation
- stop fighting
- get a date
- break up an unproductive relationship
- make a good relationship better

20. Which of the following emotional needs or desires would you like to be able to express?

- tell someone you're angry
- show that you're afraid of something
- cry or talk about something that hurt you
- admit to being bored
- tell someone something you've been keeping to yourself
- get over being resentful or jealous
- get over feeling guilty
- develop the skill to control your feelings better
- tell someone about your feelings of happiness or love
- share your dreams for the future

21. Which of the following skills would you like to develop?

- become more perceptive
- make fewer mistakes due to inattention
- improve memory
- spot problems and opportunities sooner
- develop deeper concentration
- build a more positive outlook
- become more creative
- make sounder decisions
- plan things better
- foresee more problems in advance

22. Which of the following spiritual needs would you like to fill?

- feel more in touch with reality

- develop a clearer picture of who you are
- develop a better idea of why you're here
- distinguish your inner self from your quirks and behavior
- overcome fear of growing old and dying
- overcome fear of pain and suffering
- sense the goodness in people, regardless of what they do
- overcome feelings of being better or worse than others
- experience more of the beauty of nature

23. Which of the following things do you want to do for other people?

- help a child develop and grow up properly
- help your spouse or loved one find success and happiness
- help relatives or friends achieve their goals
- improve conditions in your community
- raise money for a local charity
- serve the needs of a group, association, or committee
- contribute to society through your work
- improve conditions in your region, state, or nation
- help make the world a better place

24. What small things need to happen if you are to reach the big goals you thought about in Questionnaire A?

Once you've gone through the two questionnaires, develop your list of things you want or need. Never mind, for now, where these things are going to come from.

Photocopy the "Master List of Things I Want" shown on page 198. Under the subheading for long-term goals and desires, list the six things you want most. To develop this short list, review your notes from Questionnaire A. Don't write down a lot of items here; focus on the basic desires that are most important to you.

Under the subheading for Short-term wants and needs, list several specific things you desire in the near future. Include things you could get in the months, weeks, days, or hours ahead. This list can include as many items as you want. Review your notes from Questionnaire B to develop your list. If this list is long, you might want to organize it by categories (career, home, health, etc.) or by time (this month, this year, etc.). Date your entries if that will help.

Your list of long-term goals and desires will help you focus on what really matters to you. It is a good idea to share these goals with other people. However, other people cannot give these things to you, at least not all at once.

Your list of more concrete, short-term desires will help you decide what to go after now, and how to ask for specific assistance.

MASTER LIST OF THINGS I WANT

(Sample Worksheet)

LONG-TERM GOALS & DESIRES

_____
_____
_____
_____
_____
_____
_____
_____

SHORT-TERM WANTS & NEEDS (Use additional sheets
as needed)

_____
_____
_____
_____
_____
_____
_____
_____
_____
_____
_____
_____
_____
_____
_____

Here is a hypothetical list:

MASTER LIST OF THINGS I WANT

LONG-TERM GOALS & DESIRES

1. Own and run a successful greenhouse and nursery business. Make enough money for comfortable retirement. Help homeowners and local businesses beautify grounds and interiors. Promote gardening for more fresh fruits and vegetables.
2. Help Rachel go through college and develop her musical talent. Help her succeed either as a performer or music instructor.
3. Live up to my religious beliefs in my community and in my job as a salesman.

SHORT-TERM WANTS & NEEDS

1. Get a new or used pickup truck.
2. Get timer on VCR fixed.
3. Plan garage sale to get rid of old items and make some money.
4. Make Adam stop criticizing Michael so much; get Adam to show more respect.
5. Increase my sales for more commissions. Discuss with Rob.
6. Cut household expenses to save for greenhouse business and Rachel's college tuition.
7. Talk to Adam about changing from part-time to full-time job? (We could use the money!)
8. Plan an inexpensive summer vacation that will be fun and relaxing for everyone.

9. Get into nursery work on a part-time basis. Weekend job at a nursery? Put small greenhouse in backyard? Grow and sell one item—poinsettias? Check tax deductions possible.
10. More exercise. Swim at Y? Jog? Start doing spare-time nursery work? Build greenhouse myself?
11. Organize crew to fix retaining wall for church.
12. Build my self-image, the confidence that I can succeed.
13. Learn how to run a small business. Take a course?

STEP 2: FIGURE OUT HOW TO ASK FOR EACH THING YOU WANT

Look over your list of wants and pick one of them. Decide how to go about obtaining that thing or making it happen. Sometimes, of course, you can get what you want without help from anyone else. For example, if you want to see a movie, you can just go; or if you want to get up earlier next morning, you can simply adjust your alarm. Usually, however, you will need some help, even for satisfying relatively simple wants. For example, if you want to see a movie with someone else, obviously you'll have to ask that person. If you have trouble getting up in the morning, it might help to ask someone to give you a little encouragement.

Make notes to help you figure out how to ask for what you want. Photocopy the "Worksheet for Asking" shown on page 202. Write in the item you want at the top of the photocopied form. Then consider the ten rules of asking. How do these rules apply to getting the item in question?

Depending on the thing you want, some rules may be very important, others less important. As you think about each rule, jot down notes that will help you become more successful in getting your requests fulfilled.

WORKSHEET FOR ASKING

*WHAT I WANT IS*_____

1. What do I *really* want?_____

2. Who should I approach for help?_____

3. How can I make the best case?_____

4. What can I give in this situation?_____

5. How can I overcome my barriers to asking?_____

6. How can I ask "artfully"?_____

7. How can I avoid demanding or begging?_____

8. How can I show respect?_____

9. How can I be sure to *ask*, and keep asking?_____

10. How can I go beyond "me" to "we"?_____

Here are three examples:

Example 1:

WHAT I WANT IS: To get the timer on the VCR fixed.

1. Get it fixed.
2. Ask Jessica to get it fixed; she's old enough.
3. Tell her she'll be able to get to it sooner than her mother or I. And she's the one who uses it.
4. Don't make her feel guilty. Make it easy for her by telling her where to take it, and letting her use the station wagon.
5. My feeling is "Dad should be doing it." Nonsense!
6. Ask her in a light, upbeat way.
7. Be careful not to force her. Let her know she can say no, but the consequence will be that the timer doesn't get fixed for a while.
8. Thank her in advance for saving me time. I really don't have much time to spare.
9. Don't put it off; ask her tonight.
10. She needs confidence-building for handling things like this. Show I care about her; I'm not just trying to trick her into something.

Example 2:

WHAT I WANT IS: To increase my sales for more commissions. Discuss with Rob.

1. Increase annual income by 20 percent. Get Rob to approve a lead-generation program, so I can call on more people I know are interested.

2. Rob, since he's my manager.

3. Show how the lead-generation program can work. Do my homework first; put it in writing. If he hesitates, propose a small test program to start.

4. Make it clear how good he'll look as a manager if my sales go up 20 percent or more. Agree to help the other reps implement the program in their territories.

5. I'm afraid he might say no. Danger is I will over-prepare and put off bringing it up. Rehearse my approach with George or Karen. Approach him in stages. First let him know I'm working on a way to increase my sales by 20 percent.

6. Straightforward approach is best here. Might get George to back me up, though.

7. Present the plan as an opportunity. Don't try to push him into anything. Treat his objections, if any, as legitimate concerns. Get the facts and answer all objections.

8. Let him know how much the extra income will mean to me. In my attitude, don't forget to get across "please" and "thanks."

9. Talk to him by next Friday. In case this approach doesn't work, keep going for some way to boost income 20 percent.

10. Show Rob I'm a team player. Be careful not to one-up the other reps. Share approach with them; let Rob take credit.

Example 3:

WHAT I WANT IS: To organize a crew to fix the retaining wall for church.

1. Get stones of wall back in place. Find cause of heaving; install drainage pipes? Restore landscaping; plant ivy or rosebushes?
2. Jim, Elliott, Floyd, Ernesto, Bud, maybe Janet. Reverend Smith—ask who else might help? Ask Cerbo Nursery for good price on rosebushes or ivy. Ask for donations to cover cost.
3. Work up good spiel to use on the guys: Wall needs fixing before winter; church can't afford to hire professionals; etc.
4. Make job seem like fun. Provide soft drinks, sandwiches. If it's a game day, tell them I'll bring along my portable TV. (Ask Bud to bring his battery TV.)
5. Why have I put this off? Afraid of not getting cooperation, I guess. Maybe team up with Jim. Ask him to make calls along with me.
6. Tell everybody I got a spiritual inspiration and easily figured out who could best help me fix the wall.
7. Be willing to take no for an answer; but ask forthrightly. Let them know I really want their help; but don't sound needy. Don't plead; and don't lay a guilt trip on them.
8. Let them know, in advance, how much the church and I appreciate their sacrificing the better part of a day.
9. This Sunday is my deadline. Talk to everybody before Sunday night.
10. The job can be fun or a chore; that depends on me. And remember, the spirit of pulling together is more important than getting the wall fixed. The real church is people, not the building or the grounds.

I'm not suggesting you jot down notes for everything you want. Do it for six, twelve, or more items, enough to help you build better habits in making requests. Then, in the future, review the rules in your head before asking for anything important.

Here is an example of how my friend and associate, Dennis Allen, applied the rules of asking—in his head—to get something most of us want: a raise in salary.

Denny is an executive in the King Features syndicate. Formerly he was president of the Cowles Syndicate, which was sold to King.

It was when he was president of Cowles that he asked for a raise. Denny knew what he really wanted (Rule #1): a substantial increase in salary. He also knew who to approach (Rule #2); since he was the top man in the syndicate, only the board of directors could authorize an increase.

Denny applied Rule #3 (prepare a good case) quite thoroughly. He knew it would be a mistake to talk about "needing" more money; it would be more convincing to emphasize his increased value to the organization. "I brought my complete salary history to that meeting," he told me, "as well as a list of the financial history of the company." The second document was the more important. "I was able to chart how well the company had been doing under my leadership." He pointed out that revenues and profits had increased appreciably, while his salary had remained the same.

Another rule Denny hit hard was #4 (put giving into your asking). Over many months, he qualified himself for the raise by giving his all to the syndicate, acquiring new features and placing columns in more and more newspapers. "What it boiled down to," he said, "is that I had done my 'asking' during the previous year and a half; and now was the time for them to give me an answer."

Denny had no real barrier to asking, just a bit of nervousness that he overcame by talking about it with his wife (Rule #5). An unusual or clever approach (Rule #6) was not needed in this case.

Denny presented his request confidently and without apology (Rule #7): "I was not demanding the raise," he said, "but I was firm in establishing the need, based on my performance, for action." He showed the board due respect (Rule #8), did not hesitate to ask (Rule #9), and took care to be friendly and to create a feeling of rapport (Rule #10).

They gave him a hefty increase.

STEP 3: MAKE A SPECIAL POINT OF ASKING FOR THINGS IN THE NEAR FUTURE

Once you've made a list of the things you want, and once you've reviewed the rules of asking for some of those wants, make a special point of approaching people for the next four, eight, or more weeks.

For some of your wants, make notes on paper as you review the ten rules of asking. As you gain skill in applying the rules, you can dispense with paper and pencil. Go over the rules in your head to help decide how to ask for what you need or desire. From time to time, revise or update your list—long-range goals as well as more specific, shorter-term desires and needs.

Plan to ask, and to ask effectively. That's the main thing. It might help to use a calendar or slips of paper to "schedule" things to ask for. Jot down reminders, and act on them.

• *Suppose you want more responsibility in your job:* You can almost surely have it! Decide specifically what new duties or authority you want (Rule #1). Approach your boss or whoever can say "yes" (Rule #2). Plan your proposition in advance, maybe put it in writing (Rule #3). Figure out what your boss has to gain, such as a better-run department, or fewer worries, and plan to include these benefits in your request (Rule #4). If fear, resentment, or other feelings stand in your way, get rid of them or get around them (Rule #5). Figure out a clever way to ask, if that will impress your boss (Rule #6). Take care not to whine for the new responsibility, or bark for it (Rule #7). Thank the boss for considering your request (Rule #8). If you've put off asking, hesitate no longer; if you've been turned down before, don't let that stand in your way (Rule #9). Before asking for the responsibility, create an atmosphere of mutual trust and common purpose (Rule #10).

• *Suppose you want to invite someone special to the movies or a party:* You have an excellent chance of getting them to say "yes"! First be sure you know what you really want. Is it friendship, romance, good conversation? Decide what you want, and plan to communicate the right message (Rule #1). Approach the person you really want to be with, not just someone you can count on to say "yes" (Rule #2). Plan what to say or how to approach the person; rehearse if that will help (Rule #3). What does the other person have to gain from being with you? Think about that, and make sure your true pluses come across (Rule #4). If you're nervous about asking, or if low self-esteem stands in your way, talk to someone about it; get over your blocks to asking (Rule #5). If a clever, funny, or witty invitation will break the ice, use it (Rule #6). Ask with full self-confidence; don't come across either as a big cheese or a humble beggar (Rule #7). Put lots of consideration into your invitation; make the person feel you value and appreciate his or her company (Rule #8). Pop the question if you really like the person, even if you've been turned down before (Rule #9). Try to create a situation in which you both feel good about one another, then ask (Rule #10).

No matter what you want or need, consider the ten rules, one by one. Then apply them when you ask. You may not get a "yes" in every instance, but over time you'll receive enough positive responses to make your life richer, deeper, and more joyful.

Here is a brief summary of the ten rules that can change your life.

THE TEN RULES OF ASKING

• **Rule #1   Know What You Really Need or Want.**
If you know what to ask for, you're more likely to get it.

Set definite lifetime goals. Polish your periscope. Hitch your wagon to a star.

Ask life, or other people, for that which truly delights, empowers, or helps you grow.

Dream big and dream small. Ask for the moon. Dream of the mountaintop and put on your climbing boots.

• Rule #2   Ask the Right Person.

You can't get honey from a cow, or milk from a bee. Who has the means, knowledge, desire, or time to answer your request?

Don't seek a handout from strangers when there are hands and hearts nearer to home.

Never approach an "organization"—approach someone inside the organization.

Don't scoff at approaching intermediaries. They're important too; treat them that way.

• Rule #3   Prepare a Good Case.

Those you approach will more surely sign on the dotted line if *you* first dot your i's and mind your p's and q's.

Write your letter, and plan your approach. Then, like an actor, rehearse and refine. Would *you* buy your act?

Unlike an actor, play yourself. Be truthful and sincere. And be specific.

• Rule #4   Give in Order to Receive.

Give appreciation, give credit, give understanding, give the other person the right to say no.

Give opportunity, the possibility of profit if you're suggesting a joint venture, a prepayment of better work if you're asking for a raise.

Give inspiration, give respect. But give.

- **Rule #5   Overcome the Blocks to Asking.**

Remember, asking for things is normal; it is the way things get done.

Don't hold back. *Ask!* Though your knees are shaking, hold your head high.

You *deserve* to ask; you're expected to ask; people are depending on you to ask. If you fear you're imposing, remember—you're serving a cause.

When you're rejected, keep asking. Never give up.

- **Rule #6   Ask Artfully.**

Ask through a gesture, ask with a smile, ask by example. Use humor, use tact, use feeling, use fact.

Have someone ask for you, ask for yourself, or sneak up on the question.

Frame a question that leans toward a "yes."

- **Rule #7   Request or Invite; Never Demand or Beg.**

Never ask from weakness, even if you're down and out. Never ask with a sledgehammer, even if you've got one.

Asking should be done of equals, by equals, and for equals. You are no worse than the giver, and no better. Show it in your asking.

Make a proposal, ask for a hand, issue an invitation.

- **Rule #8   Show Respect.**

Happy endings warrant applause. Say "thank you." Make the person who grants your request smile and know they're appreciated. Reward every "no" with sincere thanks. "Thanks for your time," "Thanks for your consideration," "Thanks for your concern."

When asking for things, say thanks in advance; it

has a nice ring. When you've been wrong and have learned a lesson, say so. People see strength in those willing to reform.

Show respect in word and deed. Make sure you look good, in person and in print. And remember: Saying "please" never goes out of style. Make eye contact, shake hands firmly, show good posture, conserve the other person's time.

• Rule #9   Ask . . . And Keep Asking.

Asking works only if you do it. So do it! Ask in little ways and big ways; make it a habit.

Remember that "no" is often par for the course. Tee off again, and again. Ask—and ask again—until you succeed.

• Rule #10   Go Beyond "Me" to "We."

Forge a human connection. Let the flame of common understanding spring to life between you.

Keep asking, and you're almost sure to get results. And you won't need me to urge you on any more. Your successes will be your coach and cheering section. So go on—ask for the moon!

Chapter 14

More Than
the Moon

I began this book by telling you about how I asked for the moon and got it; and I said you could too. In Chapter 12 I talked about the "we" force that can blast you off to the moon and beyond. I'm going to end this book by coming back to earth.

William O. Douglas once said: "I hope to be remembered as someone who made the earth a little more beautiful."

Henry Miller said: "The world goes on because a few men in every generation believe in it utterly, accept it unquestioningly; they underwrite it with their lives."

William Faulkner said: "What's wrong with this world is, it's not finished yet. It is not completed to that point where man can put his final signature to the job and say, 'It is finished. We made it, and it works.'"

I say: The world is our mutual work of art. Shall we join together to complete it?

Asking is like a paintbrush that creates. It is a tool that can make our fondest dreams take shape in reality.

Asking—though a small, humble thing to do—can make big things happen.

A black woman in the South, Rosa Parks, asked for a seat up front in a bus. That ignited the final stage of the civil rights movement of the 1960s.

Jesus asked twelve men to change their occupations and follow him. His request changed history.

In the first chapter I mentioned that my family couldn't afford a bicycle for me when I was growing up. I asked my father for one, and he glanced away. Well, I asked again. "As soon as I can afford one, Percy, I'll get you one," he told me more than once. I remember the look on his face when he put me off; it was a mixture of guilt and sadness. Like other fathers, he would have loved to surprise his son with a shiny new two-wheeler; and he felt bad because most of the other boys in town had bikes. One problem was that if he somehow managed to get a bike for me, my two younger brothers would have wanted bikes too. And he certainly couldn't afford two other bikes.

One day I arrived home from school and suddenly, there it was—the bike I came to love. It was third-hand, beat-up, with two flat tires, but I was delighted! "I'll try to get bikes for your brothers, next year," my father said.

"Don't worry, Dad," I replied, "I'll share."

I asked for a bicycle—and I got one! But this is not the end of the story.

As I grew up and went into business, I always had a soft spot for kids without bikes. When I was in my twenties, I lived next door to a little boy that I liked. And, wouldn't you know, his parents couldn't afford to buy him a bike. So one Saturday I went to the local hardware store and blew half a paycheck, $25, for a surprise. You should have seen that kid jump up and down—he was my friend for life. But *this* is not the end of the story.

Over the years, as I saved money and became affluent, I gave away bike after bike—about 100 in all, up to the year 1977.

Then in 1977 I was looking for a way to brighten the lives of underprivileged children in Minneapolis. I decided to throw a Christmas party for them—a gala get-together for more than 1,000 impoverished kids of all races who never owned a bike. I would serve them refreshments in a large auditorium. I would tell them they could succeed, as I had. I would give them silver dollars as symbols of a richer future. And I would give them bicycles—a shiny new bike for each and every kid.

My assistants and I hid the bikes behind a gigantic curtain. Then, when the celebration reached a climax, the curtain went up. You should have heard the gasps, the shouts, the cheers, the gleeful screaming as those kids gazed upon 1,050 brand-spanking-new two-wheelers neatly parked in rows. Then they scrambled toward the bikes, touching them, sitting on them, riding them around joyfully.

That day I thought of my father. It was because of his influence and caring that I had reached out in my life.

The day after the bike party—Christmas morning, 1977—my phone rang. "Hello, Percy?" I recognized the voice; it was my longtime acquaintance and friend, Hubert Humphrey. Just a few weeks earlier President Jimmy Carter and Vice President Walter Mondale brought Hubert back home to Minnesota in *Air Force One*, so he could peacefully live out his life. He was dying of cancer.

He had two reasons for wanting to talk with me. I had recently given his wife, Muriel, a hand when their icemaker had gone kaput just as family was coming for Christmas. I found a new icemaker and had it delivered. From his sickbed, Hubert was calling me now, making the effort to say "thank you"!

He also wanted to tell me how moved he was by the bicycle party. He had seen a news clip about it on TV. From his sickbed he took pains to praise and encourage. What a man!

"Percy," he said, "don't be surprised if as a result of your party you get letters from people all over the country asking for help and advice. You may want to consider using a newspaper column like 'Dear Abby' or 'Ann Landers' as a way to spread your philosophy of sharing and caring."

That was the start of my "Thanks a Million" column and my writing career. The former vice president's selfless enthusiasm helped to launch me on a wider voyage of philanthropy.

We talked on for nearly an hour, reminiscing about old times, both of us breaking down and crying. Then, just before hanging up, he said, "Oh, I'll never forget seeing those kids on TV receiving those bikes. My God! Joy! Joy! Joy! Thanks a million, old buddy, and take care!" Three weeks later he died. Hubert, without knowing it, also had given me the title for my column: "Thanks a Million." But this is still not the end of the story.

Like Martin Luther King, Jr., I, too, have a dream. I'd like to give another bicycle party before I die— this one somewhere in the Middle East. I'd invite children from Israel, Egypt, Iran, Syria, Lebanon, and other countries in that eye-for-an-eye region that breeds so much distrust and terrorism. There will be gifts, games, and a bicycle for each child; but the biggest gift will be a demonstration of youthful brotherhood. The relationship between young Jews and young Arabs will determine the kind of Middle East that emerges in the next generation.

So far the foreign embassies haven't been very encouraging. Such a party would involve sensitive negotiations and would be very difficult to stage without incident. I'll have to do a lot of pushing and a lot of asking to pull it off; but I'm more than willing. In fact, I'm determined.

Why? Because I know what it's like to grow up in a world of poverty, distrust, prejudice and pain.

One time I asked for a job shining shoes, and was turned away. I was nine when the exclusive Miscowaubik Club was looking for a boy to shine shoes at a nickel a pair. My mother dressed me in my best clothes. I remember my dad even dressed up before taking me there.

My father drove me in his horse-drawn junk wagon. I remember even now how nervous I was sitting beside him on the high wooden seat. We didn't talk much and I've often wondered if he was quiet that day because he suspected what might happen when I knocked on the door of the club. Its members were the wealthier families in town, the captains and lieutenants of the Calumet and Hecla Consolidated Copper Mining Company. Even the name of the company awed and intimidated me.

As I sat on the wooden seat beside my father, jostling up and down, I saw the Miscowaubik Club come into view. It was imposing and yet elegant. My father waited while I walked to the big front door; I remember the brass handle on it. With beating heart and high hopes, I knocked. The door opened, and a well-dressed man, probably the manager, peered down at me. He didn't invite me in. He just asked what I wanted. I said, "My name is Percy Ross, and I've heard you need someone to shine shoes." He replied coolly, "We don't need boys like you."

The words hit me like a ton of bricks. Dazed, I walked back to the horse and wagon. My father was so quiet, so very quiet. I didn't know what to think at the time. Why was I turned away? Maybe it was because I was Jewish. Maybe it was because I was from the other side of the tracks: painted in large letters on the side of my father's wagon were the words WM. ROSS—JUNK DEALER.

On the ride back home, the horse's hooves hit the street like hammers on my soul. I asked my father, "Why didn't he let me in the door? . . . Why don't they want boys like me? . . . What kind of boy am I?" My father didn't have any answers. I remember I cried all the way home.

I have gotten over many disappointments, rebuffs, and injuries in my life, but the wound I received that day still hurts. It is this wound that sparked the dream of having a bicycle party in the Middle East.

I'm going to give that party for the hope, however faint, of a world without hate, fear, oppression, or resignation. I think it can make a difference. And in the depths of my heart I'm going to dedicate that party to my mother who bore me and built my confidence, to Mr. Davis who gave me a job instead of a jail sentence, to Kid Cann who extended a hand when others wrote me off, to a long line of other people who helped and encouraged me, to Hubert Humphrey who with his next to last breath cheered me on, and especially to my father, the magnificent junk dealer who gave me steel for my spine and burnished Calumet copper for my pride.

I am moved to give because I once asked, was refused, asked again, and received. Asking has changed my life; asking has given me more inner strength than you can imagine.

Asking can do at least as much for you. I'm just a grown-up poor boy, and look what I've done and may yet do!

You are as important and powerful as anyone alive. A little asking on your part can trickle like a spring, ripple like a brook, and roar like a river.

There's still so much to do! There are people to help, spirits to bolster, dreams to ignite! As Faulkner said, the world isn't finished yet. Although I'm now seventy, I intend to make the very best use of my remaining time on this earth.

I've vowed to give away my wealth, every penny, before I die. I'm still giving—and, my friend, I'm still asking!

TAKE CONTROL OF YOUR LIFE

The Ultimate Secrets of TOTAL SELF-CONFIDENCE
by Dr. Robert Anthony

Join thousands of people who have discovered THE ULTIMATE SECRETS OF TOTAL SELF-CONFIDENCE. Your career, financial situation, family life, love relationships, mental and physical health, and day to day happiness are all under y<u>our</u> control. For the first time, Dr. Robert Anthony reveals the formulas he has taught in seminars and workshops which have worked so well. Now they can work for you.

_____ **The Ultimate Secrets of Total Self-Confidence**
0-425-09143-0 $3.50
Price may be slightly higher in Canada.

Please send the titles I've checked above. Mail orders to:

BERKLEY PUBLISHING GROUP
390 Murray Hill Pkwy., Dept. B
East Rutherford, NJ 07073

NAME_____

ADDRESS_____

CITY_____

STATE_____ ZIP_____

Please allow 6 weeks for delivery.
Prices are subject to change without notice.

POSTAGE & HANDLING: $1.00 for one book, $.25 for each additional. Do not exceed $3.50.	
BOOK TOTAL	$_____
SHIPPING & HANDLING	$_____
APPLICABLE SALES TAX (CA, NJ, NY, PA)	$_____
TOTAL AMOUNT DUE PAYABLE IN US FUNDS. (No cash orders accepted.)	$_____

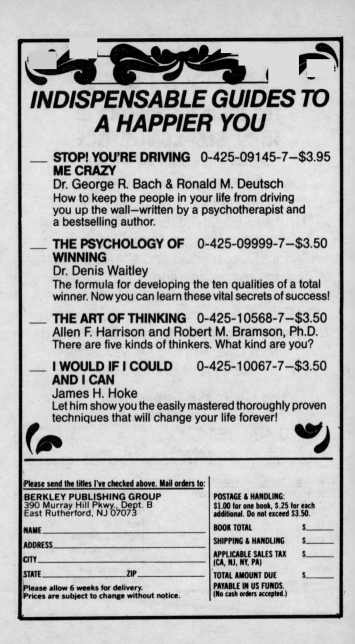

INDISPENSABLE GUIDES TO A HAPPIER YOU

___ **STOP! YOU'RE DRIVING**   0-425-09145-7—$3.95
ME CRAZY
Dr. George R. Bach & Ronald M. Deutsch
How to keep the people in your life from driving
you up the wall—written by a psychotherapist and
a bestselling author.

___ **THE PSYCHOLOGY OF**   0-425-09999-7—$3.50
WINNING
Dr. Denis Waitley
The formula for developing the ten qualities of a total
winner. Now you can learn these vital secrets of success!

___ **THE ART OF THINKING**   0-425-10568-7—$3.50
Allen F. Harrison and Robert M. Bramson, Ph.D.
There are five kinds of thinkers. What kind are you?

___ **I WOULD IF I COULD**   0-425-10067-7—$3.50
AND I CAN
James H. Hoke
Let him show you the easily mastered thoroughly proven
techniques that will change your life forever!

Please send the titles I've checked above. Mail orders to:

BERKLEY PUBLISHING GROUP
390 Murray Hill Pkwy., Dept. B
East Rutherford, NJ 07073

NAME _____

ADDRESS _____

CITY _____

STATE _____ ZIP _____

Please allow 6 weeks for delivery.
Prices are subject to change without notice.

POSTAGE & HANDLING:
$1.00 for one book, $.25 for each
additional. Do not exceed $3.50.

BOOK TOTAL $_____

SHIPPING & HANDLING $_____

APPLICABLE SALES TAX $_____
(CA, NJ, NY, PA)

TOTAL AMOUNT DUE $_____
PAYABLE IN US FUNDS.
(No cash orders accepted.)

"Nido Qubein has captured the wisdom of many of the greatest thinkers and doers of all time!"
—Norman Vincent Peale

AMERICA'S SUPER SALESMAN
Shows You the Way to Personal and Professional Success!

— NIDO QUBEIN'S PROFESSIONAL SELLING TECHNIQUES
0-425-07653-9/$5.95 **(Large Format)**

With today's tight economy, cost-conscious consumers, and fierce competition, it takes a new kind of professional to succeed in selling. Now Nido Qubein reveals the secrets of selling to today's tough sophisticated market—and shows you how to reap the huge rewards belonging to the salesperson who can meet today's challenges!

— GET THE BEST FROM YOURSELF 0-425-08537-6/$3.50

"Winners are made—not born!" So make yourself into a winner with Nido Qubein's complete program for self-fulfillment. Learn to develop a positive self-image...become a leader...handle stress...turn problems into adventures...And make your dreams come true!

Please send the titles I've checked above. Mail orders to:

BERKLEY PUBLISHING GROUP
390 Murray Hill Pkwy., Dept. B
East Rutherford, NJ 07073

NAME _____

ADDRESS _____

CITY _____

STATE _____ ZIP _____

Please allow 6 weeks for delivery.
Prices are subject to change without notice.

POSTAGE & HANDLING:
$1.00 for one book, $.25 for each additional. Do not exceed $3.50.

BOOK TOTAL $_____

SHIPPING & HANDLING $_____

APPLICABLE SALES TAX $_____
(CA, NJ, NY, PA)

TOTAL AMOUNT DUE $_____
PAYABLE IN US FUNDS.
(No cash orders accepted.)

Top Performance

ZIG ZIGLAR

THE BESTSELLING AUTHOR OF
ZIG ZIGLAR'S SECRETS
OF CLOSING THE SALE
REVEALS MORE
SECRETS IN GAINING
UNBEATABLE RESULTS!

HOW TO DEVELOP EXCELLENCE IN YOURSELF AND OTHERS

**"To call Zig Ziglar a 'super salesman'
would be an understatement."**
— RICHARD M. DeVOS, PRESIDENT, AMWAY CORPORATION

America's #1 motivator shows you the formulas, principles and
techniques that will take you to the top!

★ 17 maxims to unlock top performance
★ 10 commandments for running a meeting
★ 5 management myths that should be exploded
★ 6 key work attitudes
★ 22 principles to meet a person's needs
★ The 7-step goal setting formula
★ 3 ways to build healthy self-esteem
★ And much more!

__**TOP PERFORMANCE: HOW TO DEVELOP**   0-425-09973-3/$7.95
EXCELLENCE IN YOURSELF AND OTHERS (trade edition)

Available at your local bookstore or return this form to:

THE BERKLEY PUBLISHING GROUP
Berkley • Jove • Charter • Ace
THE BERKLEY PUBLISHING GROUP, Dept. B
390 Murray Hill Parkway, East Rutherford, NJ 07073

Please send me the titles checked above. I enclose _____ Include $1.00 for postage
and handling if one book is ordered; add 25¢ per book for two or more not to exceed
$1.75. CA, NJ, NY and PA residents please add sales tax. Prices subject to change
without notice and may be higher in Canada. Do not send cash.

NAME_____

ADDRESS_____

CITY_____ STATE/ZIP_____

(Allow six weeks for delivery.)   B504